To Best friend and Companion

Phyllis,

The memories we share are so
wonderful. thanks and enjoy the book—

Walter H Daniels MD

THE MAN AND THE DOCTOR

Walter H. Daniels, M.D.

ISBN: 1539120570
ISBN 13: 9781539120575
Library of Congress Control Number: 2016916400
CreateSpace Independent Publishing Platform
North Charleston, South Carolina

CONTENTS

PREFACE

I cannot recall when I first realized that I wanted to write a book, but my joining and participating in a Life Writing class has allowed me to admit and complete that desire in a joyful manner with reflections on my personal life and as a doctor. I have compiled memories from my childhood in a small Cajun town in south Louisiana with a story revealing my intentions to become a doctor by operating on my pet skunk (Poowee and Oohwee), as well as medical school tales of fishing cadavers (Body Movers). I've included stories from my experiences as a family doctor, travel adventures with my wife Pam, and ghost stories about our plantation home, Idlewild.

All of the people I mention in my stories are real people but most of the time not their real names.

THE EARLY YEARS

***

MY CAJUN MOTHER

My mother, Delta Fruge', was of French descent, with some of her ancestors coming directly from France and some via the Grand Derangement (the Great Migration) from Nova Scotia. Her father and mother settled in Gueydan, Louisiana, after having moved from Abbeville. She and her four siblings were fluently bilingual, although her mother spoke only French.

Mother moved up the social and financial ladder at age eighteen when she married an oilfield worker, Homer Daniels, who migrated with the oil boom from West Texas. The oil men all earned excellent wages in relation to the poor rice farming Cajuns and were looked up to because of that, as well as being English speaking Americans. She and my father lived in the Pure Oil Camp, a six house compound, five miles out of town, inhabited by other migrant oil workers.

Although she was residing outside the local Cajun community, Mother maintained a close bond with her family, visiting them at least weekly when she attended the Catholic Church for Sunday mass. My mother's personality and accommodating spirit was the major factor that allowed her and my father to have such a happy marriage for so many years. He was a Methodist and would not be married in a Catholic ceremony, so Mother allowed a legal ceremony, although this prevented her from being able to receive communion. She was a devout Catholic and my father's refusal to have the marriage blessed in the Catholic Church caused recurring friction. His reason for the continued refusal was that getting married again would be inferring that the original marriage was not valid, which would imply they have been living unmarried all of these years and that their two sons were illegitimate bastards. Despite this, Mother continued a loving and religious relationship while attending mass every Sunday and received communion the first Sunday after he died.

Mother was always the lubricant that made the family run smoothly. She was the caretaker of my brother, Carly and I, always ensuring that we were well nourished, attending school, making good grades and living in a spotless house. She was also our primary disciplinarian. When we did anything wrong, there was always punishment. If we were outside, she would cut a switch branch off a small tree and use it to chastise us. If we were inside, the punishment was inflicted by the palm of her hand on our buttocks. Rarely did Daddy ever punish us, and only when the wrongdoing was directly associated with him, and it was a major whipping with his horsehide belt, made in the Texas State Prison.

Surprisingly she was not a very good cook, although food at all meals was plentiful. Sunday noon was the main meal and our favorite dish was fried chicken, which was her best. Preparation was quite a chore, but so important that we maintained a small chicken coop holding three or four chickens inside it. When it was time, she would reach inside the coop, grasp a chicken by the neck, and then ring it until it broke and drop it to the ground. When it quit flopping, she would place it in a bucket of hot water to soak and make the plucking easier. After dismembering the bird, she soaked it in egg batter and flour, then frying it to a crisp.

Mother was aware of the value of money, a residual of her days raised in poverty, and she was always using any means of earning a few dollars. The longest lasting was processing the milk obtained daily by my milking our Jersey milk cow. I would bring in at least two gallons every morning. She would then strain it, place most of it in quart milk bottles with a cap and give it to me to deliver to the other neighbors who paid for it weekly. Any leftover milk was saved and once a week she would get out her churn and make homemade butter, which sold quickly.

Her other money maker was to make honey available when Daddy robbed his beehives. She would harvest the honey from the slats, remove the comb from some, and then place it in jars of various sizes. After washing the honey from the outside of the jars, she would take it to town where she sold it to the various grocery stores. It was always quickly sold.

Saturday afternoon was the shopping and social time in Gueydan, when the oilfield workers and farmers all came to town. In a four block area of Main Street was a grocery store, picture show, doctor's office, drug store and four saloons. Lulu's bar was my Dad's favorite, which he visited to drink beer and play poker. He was known for his gambling skill and almost always brought home winnings. Mother would drop him off and with my brother and me in tow, go grocery shopping and visit her mother and siblings. She and Daddy would have a time set when she would return to Lulu's and he would meet her outside and we would return home.

Mother's strong personality and fortitude showed through the last time this happened. She had completed her shopping and visiting and we drove up and parked in front of Lulu's, not to find Daddy waiting outside. Sometime later, she stopped her cousin Elias before he entered the old saloon half door and asked him to tell Dad that we were waiting outside. Still no Dad. It became obvious after a while that Mother was running out of patience. She could not go in and get him, as the only females in bars were those of poor reputation. Then surprisingly she directed me.

"Go in there and tell your Daddy that I am tired of waiting, and he should come out so we can go home. He will be in the small poker room." Knowing that a twelve-year-old would not be allowed in a bar, she continued. "If Otto the bartender says anything, tell him that I sent you in there to get your Daddy."

I entered the saloon and before Otto could say anything I explained what was happening. Inside a smoke-filled room, beside the side of the serving bar was my Dad with four of his poker playing buddies. Immediately after spying me, he threw his cards on the table, swigged the remainder of his beer, picked up his money and took my hand as we walked out and entered the car.

Before Mother could say a word, he said, "I'm sorry I'm late and you had to wait but I was having a run of good luck and I figured your time was worth this," as he handed her twenty-five dollars, two hundred fifty in today's money. Recognizing the gasoline that ran the family, Mother accepted the money without saying a word.

Mother's education was limited as she only completed the seventh grade, however, she was a prodigious and knowledgeable reader, belonging to clubs and borrowing and buying books. Having little education always shamed her and when her son became a doctor, she enrolled in school and obtained her G.E.D. This gave her pride and status that she had missed all of these years in comparison to her youngest sister, who was her class Valedictorian.

My mother had always dreamed of traveling, but was limited to my father's dislike of it. He only traveled to his work areas in South Louisiana and to his siblings in Texas. Mother had been limited to Louisiana, Texas and Mississippi until after my father's demise, when one of her friends talked her into a vacation trip to Hawaii. That ended up being a highlight of her life and everyone heard the details anytime they were around her. With a little encouragement, she would even demonstrate the Hula.

Dedication was one of the strong attributes of my mother which became even more apparent as my father became older and less able to be independent. She filled his needs in the most unobtrusive manner without his requests by using her knowledge of him gained by all of their years together. Part of her life ended along with him and she lost her feeling of usefulness for the remainder of her days.

MY FIRST BEDROOM

The first home I remember was where I was born. My mother told me the story of my birth in our home at the Pure Oil Camp when 'Old Doc' drove the five miles from Gueydan to attend the birth. Upon completion of the birth, he held me aloft and said, "This boy weighs about seven pounds," and this was entered on my birth certificate, which he completed and gave to my parents on site.

Our house was one of six in the compound, five of which were alike, with five rooms and one bath. The superintendent's house was slightly larger with three bedrooms. All had an open front porch and ours had a swing, seating two people. On one side of the house entering off the porch was the living room where most of our time was spent when not eating or sleeping. Leading from there through a room divider was the dining room where we ate only on very special occasions, once or twice a year. A small door led from there into the kitchen where mother did all the cooking. We ate all meals together there at the kitchen table seating four.

On the other side of the house through doors leading from the living room and dining room were the front and rear bedrooms. These were very simple, spartan rooms with a double bed and chest of drawers. The rear bedroom was for my parents and also contained a dresser and a small oscillating fan directly over their bed. A small bathroom separated their bedroom from the front one occupied by me and my brother, Carly.

Our bedroom contained an old iron bed for two, a small chest of drawers for our clothes and a small closet. One screened window opened onto the front porch next to the swing. Two other screened windows opened onto the side yard which was shared with neighbors about fifty feet away. The windows were essential for ventilation and our bed rested where any breeze would blow over it.

Our time in the bedroom was mainly playing in the bed near sleep time and trying to fall asleep in the heat, while listening to the fan running in my parent's bedroom. The most memorable event and memory of our bedroom was the first night when the window fan was installed. An unbelievable breeze was pulled through the windows, so cool that we had to cover with sheets.

There was little privacy in the house so rules were enforced by our parents. We were never to enter their room without knocking on the door and asking permission. The bathroom doors must be closed anytime it was in use and could never be entered without permission.

The smallness of the house allowed the travel of sound through the rooms. This didn't allow Carly and I much play time at night, as it would disturb Mother and Daddy. The squeaking mattress sound at night from the parent's room was prevalent but cause unknown in my early years.

Sounds from the bathroom in the middle of the night were also common but mysterious. I would hear my father walk into the bathroom and then sound like he was opening small packages.

One day when exploring the bathroom at an early age I learned the cause of the sound but didn't recognize it until a few years later when I learned about sex. On a shelf high in the bathroom over the toilet was a glass flower bowl in the form of a black swan. Searching inside it I found several small boxes, some empty, and learned they were "rubbers". The secret remained with me. I learned why we never had siblings.

MON CHER

Written from my perceived viewpoint of my grandmother.

I am Editha Fruge', the mother of five children and nine grandchildren. My great-great grandparents migrated to Acadia, French South Louisiana, in the early 1800's. We have always considered ourselves French-Americans, reading, writing, speaking French and maintaining the customs of our heritage.

My husband, August, and several of his brothers moved from Abbeville to Gueydan to take advantage of the job opportunities, working in rice mills and on farms. The dominant language and culture was French-Acadian, now changed to Cajun by the English speaking Texans, who invaded our area with oil and had no formal education. All daily transactions, such as purchases of goods and services, were done in French, only legal transactions required interpreters. The daily mass was in French and Latin.

All of my children were bilingual, as were my grandchildren with the exception of one. My daughter, Delta, fell for a Texas oil worker, who didn't speak French and never tried to learn it. Only English was spoken in their home and my grandson, Walter, couldn't speak French. This made it very difficult for him when his mother visited because I spoke no English. Walter wasn't a French name, so I called him "Mon Cher," My Love. His father, Homer, rarely came into my house, just dropping them off and going to work. He couldn't stand hearing the French and not comprehending.

When Walter came to spend the night with me, as I cared for him when Delta and Homer went somewhere, it was very difficult. He knew only a few basic words, as did I. Our time was spent hugging, doing sign language, pointing and eating. Walter would spend time outdoors, in and under the china ball tree. During our time together I particularly regretted our inability to communicate as I could not tell him of his ancestry, especially about my husband and his grandfather, August, who died before he was born.

I have been very proud of my children who have all done well in life despite being raised in poverty. My two sons served in World War II. The oldest, Lulu, was on a navy battleship. The other son, Oscar, served in General Patton's army in France and in the Battle of the Bulge into Germany. He became a Master Sergeant, and with his fluency in Cajun French, he was an interpreter. My youngest daughter, Gloria, graduated from Gueydan High School, number one in her class. My oldest daughter, Elite, started a grocery store and maintained it for many years. And Mon Cher's mother, Delta, dropped out of school in the seventh grade. However, when her son was in medical school she earned her GED through classes at Gueydan High.

For many years I wished Mon Cher would have learned French. Au revoir.

As grandma's favorite grandson, and her "Mon Cher," I hope she can look down and see that I am now fluent in English, German and French, and speak a few words of Spanish and Vietnamese.

MY ONLY GRANDFATHER

One rarely remembers a happening at age thirteen with much clarity sixty-five years later. The event I remember so well was the first and only visit to my paternal grandfather. I knew he was bedridden and lived in a boarding house, being informed of this situation by my father before we left on a driving trip to the small West Texas town of Mexia, to visit James Homer Daniel for perhaps the last time, as he was getting older and feebler.

The trip was very long and boring, with my brother and I sitting in the rear seat re-breathing my father's cigar smoke inside the small car.

Mexia was off the beaten track and had one street with small stores on each side. At the end of the street was an old two-story house with windows on each side, top and bottom, and peeling paint. We stopped and parked in front of the building's sign "Mexia Boarding House." My father exited the car and went inside, leaving my mother, brother and me in the car. A short time later, he returned to get me to accompany him.

The inside was very wide and dreary with high ceilings, and all wood and painted white. Seated at a desk in front of stairs at the rear of the entrance room was a lady receptionist. She nodded to my father saying, "Go upstairs to room 210 on the right. Your father, James Homer Daniel, is in that room. He is alone at this time as his caretaker is occupied with other duties at present."

We climbed up the long stairs that I remember being very steep and entered a dark hallway with doors on each side. My father led the way down to room 210 and knocked on the closed door. A hoarse, weak voice responded within with, "Come in."

We entered the small room and I remember being frightened by the old bearded man lying in a bed, with his head elevated and the strong smell surrounding him. My father walked over and grasped one of his hands.

"Dad, it's your boy, Homer, and I have come to visit you," he said.

The old man appeared startled and responded with, "Homer, it is so good to hear your voice. I can no longer see, but I remember your voice."

My father then motioned me to come next to the bed and placed my hand upon my grandfather's, saying, "This hand belongs to my son, Walter, your grandson." Tears flowed from my grandfather's eyes as he gently squeezed my hand, and I responded by kissing him on the cheek.

At my father's direction, I went downstairs to our car out front and brought my mother and brother back into Grandfather James' room. They met and greeted him and the small room became crowded and stuffy, but was filled with love and good feelings.

After several hours, it was time to depart and continue our journey to visit my father's two sisters, who lived in Fort Worth and Mineral Wells, Texas.

Leaving was quite sad and Grandfather James said, "Homer, promise me you will return to see me in a short time."

My father agreed to this request, but was unable to fulfill his promise, as Grandfather James died one month later.

MY FEET DIDN'T FIT IN HIS SHOES

For as long as I can remember, my father was a dominant factor in my life. When I first attempted to walk in his shoes, I knew I would be unsuccessful. His shoes were hard leather, hard soled, steel-toed work boots that hurt my feet.

Daddy, as my brother and I have always addressed him, had a hard early life in the early 1900s even though he was born on the Fourth of July. He was forced to drop out of school at age 14 to become the caretaker of his three younger sisters, when his father became paralyzed from polio and his mother died. He accepted any job available, all being manual labor. In the oil boom years of the early thirties he became a rig builder. He worked his way across Texas, into Louisiana and ended up in the poor Cajun town of Gueydan during the depression. His famous saying was, "I ran out of money in Gueydan and I never made enough to leave."

Daddy, because of all the hardships, was very tight fisted, never wasting a nickel, but compared to the general population in

Gueydan, made a good living as construction foreman for Pure Oil Company, later to become Humble Oil. He was always looking for another way to earn more money. He loved being a cowboy and began to buy a few cattle and a bull as well as two horses, one for him and one for me. He instilled his work ethic into me, buying a milk cow which I milked every morning and was paid one dollar and a half weekly. Mother would strain and bottle the milk and I would deliver it to the other five families at the Pure Oil Camp, where we lived. I didn't get paid for that.

As another side line to make a few more bucks, he bought a book on bee farming and began to raise bees and harvesting and preparing the honey. At one time he had eight bee hives. When they swarmed outside of the colony with a new queen, he would collect them into a new hive.

Harvesting the honey was another thing that made his shoes a tight fit. Outfitted with a screen face mask and all the rest of his body covered with clothing, his gloved hand holding the smoker, he would approach the hive, remove the lid and begin to remove the slats filled with honey. The smoker didn't keep all of the bees off of him and he always got stung by bees making their way through his clothes once or twice with no complaints. He would carve the honey out and deposit it into a large washtub, from which my mother cleaned and processed it into various sized jars. It would then be sold to neighbors and to stores in Gueydan.

To say he was a strict disciplinarian is to be very generous. To this day, I still remember the last time I disobeyed him. The Pure Oil Camp, where we lived, was five miles from Gueydan and one mile from "The Oil Lease", an aggregate of pumping wells, storage tanks and bar pits. The lease was surrounded by levees and frequently flooded. After a heavy downpour, my friend Ray and I got word that the flooding was considerable and worth seeing. We asked our Dads if we could walk down the levee and see the flood. Ray's father gave him permission, but Daddy said, "No". Ray indicated he was going without me which didn't sit right with me and I decided to sneak away.

Ray and I made the trip in an uneventful way and were walking back on the levee toward the camp, when we encountered Elias, one of the roustabouts. Looking at me he said, "Boy, you better get your butt home quickly, your Dad is looking for you."

Knowing that I was in deep trouble, I ran the remainder of the way to my house. Going to the rear of the house, I was met by Daddy sitting on the steps.

"Where have you been?" he asked.

"At the lease," I replied.

He arose saying, "Come in here," as he gestured toward the back porch. He then began to remove his prized horse-hair belt, handmade by an inmate at Texas State Prison. He was very proud of that belt. "Bend over and grab your ankles," he said.

Knowing what was approaching, I followed his directions. He then proceeded to give me five lashes on my buttocks. The last two brought cries from me. "Now pull your pants down and let me see if it's red. If it's not, you will get some more" he said.

My Mother had been observing the punishment, cried out, "Homer, please don't whip him anymore." As I slipped my trousers down, I prayed I would be red and thankfully I was.

He completed the punishment with, "If you ever disobey me again, this will be nothing." I never did and at that time, I knew I didn't want to walk in those shoes.

My Daddy was very intelligent although only getting a seventh grade education. He developed a dirt contracting business and quit working for Pure Oil. He had a drag line for digging irrigation canals. To make a bid on a project he had to measure the length, width and depth of the proposed project, then make a paper calculation of the cubic feet of dirt to be removed. He traveled all through Southwestern Louisiana doing jobs and the business grew to three draglines and then he purchased a bulldozer.

All through my high school years, my Dad would give me jobs which paid me for my productivity. He paid me to unload a box-car full of gravel by hand shovel. With that money I hired three classmates and made them work hard so I could profit. He had a hay baling machine and paid me so much a bale to load them on a truck and transport them to the farmer's barn. The more bales moved, the more money I made, so classmates were my workers. Then came the biggest job ever.

When he purchased the bulldozer, there was not another one in the Gueydan area, nor was there anyone who knew how to run one. The dozer was delivered and he took me with him to see it. It was a beautiful bright yellow, huge piece of machinery.

"Who is going to operate it?" I asked.

"You are," he replied and handed me a book titled, "Operations of a Caterpillar D-7." I was only fifteen years old and I was going to run this monster. I was excited, frightened and didn't know if my shoes were big enough, but everything worked out and I became the only bulldozer operator of the only bulldozer in the area.

My Dad was great at making me independent and disciplined so I knew he cared for me but he never expressed or showed affection to me. He was affectionate to my mother and to his sisters but never to my brother or me. He never hugged me and only shook my hand. He never attended any of the athletic contests, speech or literary rallies or any of my school functions until my graduation, which my mother made him attend. He paid my way through college and medical school, but never attended any functions until I graduated from medical school. It was shortly following, that he finally expressed that he was proud of me in an introduction to one of his friends, he said, "This is my son Walter, the Doctor." Then I knew that even though I hadn't walked in his shoes, he had influenced and purchased and was proud of the shoes I was walking in.

UNCLE LULU'S HOUSE

My pre-teen years staying with people, other than my parents, were mainly occupied by my uncles and aunts on my mother's side, as they all resided in the small Cajun town of Gueydan, while my father's side lived in Texas. Any time spent in town was mostly at Uncle Lulu's house, where my only male cousin near my age lived. This was a different lifestyle and activity than my home life.

Uncle Lulu's house was a wooden, two room Cajun house with an open front porch covered by a roof. The front yard had no grass and one "china ball" tree in which we could climb and harvest china balls for use in our "shooter" battles. The biggest use and the most fun on the bare earth was playing marbles "For Keeps." My cousin, Sheldon, was the neighborhood expert and never let me go home with any marbles.

The neighborhood was a very poor one with dirt roads and small two and three room houses, similar to Uncle Lulu's. Spending the night there was always an adventure. The inside of the house had a wood burning stove for warmth and cooking. The main room was separated from the adult's bedroom by a curtain. Sheldon and I slept on the floor in the corner of the main room. It was a hard floor.

A fun feature of staying there was going swimming every afternoon. The Rice Canal ran a short distance behind Uncle Lulu's house. Pumped water flowed through it and was very clean and clear. We would put on our bathing suits and walk down to the canal with Uncle Lulu and dive in the refreshingly cold water.

The neighborhood was always safe and happy, even with the marked poverty. In the warm spring and summer, Uncle Lulu and his Cajun neighbors' band would gather on his porch on Friday afternoon and the people nearby would gather around to be entertained.

Uncle Lulu played the fiddle and sang, "Black" Millima, the next door neighbor, played the washboard. Sam Fruge, a younger member, played the guitar and Pete Primeaux played the handle accordion, also called the "chank-a-chank." Their music was only Cajun, but entertaining enough that people sang and danced on the bare earth.

Time spent at Uncle Lulu's house was always happy and carefree within a warm, loving environment. Between the marble games, swimming, good music and great Cajun food, what else could one want?

Life was good.

UNCLE OSCAR

The favorite of all my uncles and aunts was Uncle Oscar. I suppose that was because he was the younger of my mother's two brothers, active in life and nearer my age.

Shortly after graduating from high school, in the midst of the Second World War, he enlisted in the U.S. Army and was assigned to General Patton's famous Third Army. There his Cajun heritage and bilingualism made him a very valuable soldier. One of General Patton's most famous battles was the Battle of the Bulge, which occurred in France. It was one of the most important and decisive battles of WW II. His ability to speak fluent Cajun French procured Uncle Oscar the position of a top interpreter and a Master Sergeant. He held this position throughout the entire battle.

France had been under German domination for several years when the Americans mounted their attempt to free them. The French people were so happy and thankful that they opened their homes and hearts to the American soldiers in gratitude. Being able to respond to them with," Bonjour, Je parle francais," opened many doors and made Uncle Oscar a prized friend, as he enabled close contact of his fellow soldiers with the young French maidens, and for himself. The small towns had festive occasions to facilitate these meetings, and Uncle Oscar was in great demand to teach the Cajun "two-step" dance, while speaking French. One relationship lasted through his entire tour in France, but couldn't weather the distance across the Atlantic. Letters and rare phone calls kept it breathing, but only for a short time.

Later, after completing his tour of duty, Uncle Oscar moved back to Gueydan where he met and married a very attractive lady from Jennings, Louisiana, a larger town twenty miles from Gueydan, where he moved and worked.

On rare occasions, I would visit him and Aunt Alice for a weekend, with he and Mother ferrying me back and forth. It was on one of these sojourns that I got my first glimpse of "messing around."

I was about thirteen years old when Uncle Oscar and I were taking a trip to downtown Jennings on a bus. As we entered the bus, he seated us behind the other passenger, an attractive lady. Shortly, as the bus resumed its trip, he began to speak to this lady, and after we traveled a few blocks he arose and seated himself next to her, where he remained until the bus stopped and she began to depart. Uncle Oscar arose, grasped my hand and said, "Come on Walter, we are getting off here."

"But, Uncle Oscar, this isn't your house," I answered.

"Don't worry, we are only a short distance away. We will walk the rest of the way. You wait here," he said and began to walk toward the house with the lady.

At the door, they stopped and kissed, and then Uncle Oscar returned to me saying, "Don't you dare tell anyone about this or I will whip your ass," adding emphasis by squeezing my arm.

Knowing Uncle Oscar's reputation of a fierce temper since returning from the Army, I replied, "I promise I won't tell a soul. This is a secret between us." With that, I pulled my arm and stepped away fearfully.

I never learned if anything came of this encounter, but he and Aunt Alice divorced two years later. However, as a ripening 13-year-old, it was a lesson in "making out" that I have remembered for many years. Uncle Oscar must have been a "ladies' man," as each marriage overflowed with stories of rendezvous and separations. His fifth marriage was his most successful one, and death completed it.

"I'LL TELL"

Growing up many years ago was quite different than it is today. There were no TVs, cell phones or computers and many people didn't have air conditioning. We developed our heroes from picture shows and comic books or funny books, as they were more commonly known. Cowboys were the big thing back then and everyone knew Gene Autrey, Roy Rogers and Tex Ritter for their horseback riding and shooting pistols and rifles.

When we were nine and ten my brother, Carly, and friend Ray, played cowboys. We wore toy pistols in holsters attached to belts around our waists and we would have fast-draw contests. The pistols were loaded with caps that popped when we pulled the trigger or we just yelled, "Bang! Bang! I got you."

We also played "Hide and Seek" using our guns when we found the one hiding. Usually Ray and Carly would join together looking for me. We would hide behind some object or building, where we could jump out shooting our cap pistols and yelling, "Bang Bang! I got you."

My brother, Carly, was lucky because he had a single shot pump B.B. rifle. If 'cool' had been used back then, that would have described his rifle. We all wanted one just like it. To shoot it, Carly would pull the pump lever under the gun. This opened the chamber where he would place one B.B., a small metal ball. The pump also pushed air into the rifle, which pushed the B.B. out when the trigger was pulled. When we were playing our games, Carly would never load the rifle. An unbreakable rule was to never point a loaded gun at anyone.

One day we were playing our game and I was looking for Ray and Carly. As I came around the corner of the garage, they jumped out in front of me, Ray shooting his cap pistol and Carly aiming his rifle at me and pulling the trigger.

I suddenly felt something hitting my stomach and there was a tiny hole in the bottom of my shirt. I pulled my shirt up and there was a little hole above my belly button with blood trickling from it.

"Carly, you shot me," I screamed while exaggerating the pain. "I'm going to tell Daddy."

"I didn't have a B.B. in the gun," he answered and then he saw the B.B. fall out of my shirt and he became very scared. "I'm sorry, I'm sorry," he cried. "I didn't mean to. Please don't tell Daddy. He will whip me and take my gun away."

"I'll tell," I answered and Carly began to cry in big sobs.

After a little while, I looked at Carly and said, "O.K. I won't tell, but you are going to have to do anything that I tell you to do or I'll tell. You will have to be my slave."

"I'll do anything you want as long as you don't tell," said Carly. His promise started a fun time for me. Anytime I had to do something that I didn't want to, I would tell Carly to do it. If he said no or acted like he wouldn't do it, I would say, "I'll tell," and he would immediately do the task. As time passed, Carly tried more and more to keep from obeying me, but "I'll tell" always worked.

One day, Ray and I were talking and he said to me, "You are really being mean to your brother, making him do all of those things or you will tell."

I looked at Ray and said, "I'll tell you a secret but you must promise to never tell Carly."

"I promise," he answered.

"If Carly doesn't do what I tell him to, I wouldn't tell Daddy that he shot me," I confessed.

"You wouldn't?"

"No. Daddy would be too mad and might punish me too," I said. A few days passed and it was time to mow the yard. Carly and I each had a part of the yard to mow. I was sitting in the cool shade of our oak tree and I told Carly, "You have to mow my part of the yard today or I'll tell."

He looked at me with a very mean look on his face and said, "I will not mow your part of the yard today or any day. I won't do any more things for you. I won't get the paper, fan you at night till you go to sleep, wash the dogs or anything else. You can't make me do anything anymore. If you want to tell, Tell!" I then knew that Ray had told Carly and "I'll tell" would never work again.

WHO WAS THE WINNER?

I awakened early on Saturday morning to loud voices coming from my parents' bedroom. Simple walls separated the rooms for privacy, but didn't shield the noise. Hearing voices from their bedroom was usually a worry because none of their differences were ever aired in the presence of my brother and I, and hearing their anger was always distressful.

"I don't want Walter to work on Sunday. This is sinful," said my good Catholic mother.

"If we don't take care of these cattle, we can't sell them and we won't have money for food. Sunday is the only day in the week that I can get horse riders. Walter needs to learn to herd cattle no matter what day of the week," answered my hard working, tough, Methodist father.

I was fourteen years old at the time and had heard of this conversation in the past. I didn't have a good solution, although I wanted to work for my money and the prestige of riding a horse, rounding up and caring for a herd of cattle. Being raised by parents of different religions in a mainly Catholic community sometimes was difficult.

My mother was a strong Catholic and believed in living by the rules, and she was adamantly opposed to working on a Sunday. This rule was strongly adhered to in the farming Cajun prairie town of Gueydan, except during rice harvest season when bending the rules slightly was acceptable, as necessity dictated working on Sunday. Even the Cardinal Law of attending Mass on Sunday had accommodations in planting or harvest times. A special service was held on Saturday evening and a very short one was held Sunday morning before five o'clock. These were also in effect for the most important, duck hunting season.

My father was extremely hard working and if a job was awaiting, he performed it no matter what might interfere, including my mother. He was insistent that my brother and I were also instilled with the "work no matter what ethic."

There were few recurring frictions in our family. Mother took good care of nutrition, minor discipline and house duties. Daddy brought home the money and ruled the house with an iron fist. We had a good comfortable life and I was on my horse with the other riders on Sunday.

THE THREE BROUSSARD SISTERS AND MORE

Teachers have always been held in high esteem in the Cajun country, but never more so than in my early school days of the late 30's and 40's. Their elevated position in Cajun society was not for financial or family reasons, but because of their educated status, when compared by the common man, and their aim to pass on this education.

In my little Acadian village of Gueydan, the three Broussard sisters were well known and renowned for their efforts as educators. They were natives of Gueydan, daughters of a well-to-do rice farmer, and all educated in local schools and then higher education at University of Southwestern in Lafayette, Louisiana, then returning to teach in their native village.

Madeline and Theresa, both unmarried, were known as "Old Maids", and lived in the family home, a large white house on Main Street, just two blocks from the elementary school. Mae Broussard dePerrodil lived in a fine house on the outskirts of town and was driven to school by her husband, who owned a fuel delivery service.

Madeline Broussard was a 1st Grade teacher, who was much sought after to become the teacher of new entries to the school. My mother and father were very happy when I ended up in Miss Madeline's class. In class, she was kind, warm, but insistent on learning. She cared greatly for her students as children.

I still remember an incident in her room one day when I was feeling ill. Noting this, she took me aside and said, "Walter, you stay with me and help me copy some papers for Miss Theresa's third grade reading class." As the other students went out for recess, she led me into a small room in which was a copier, then called a "Ditto machine." Here she took out some typed sheets and placed then on the Ditto machine and began to make copies. Bored, I stood next to her and attempted to read the sheets. Miss Madeline noted this and asked me if I could read this material, which was being prepared for 3rd graders. I began reading a few words aloud, but enough to impress her.

"Come with me!" she said, as she gathered up the papers and took me by the hand, leading me down the hall to Mrs. Toups, the best 2nd grade teacher in the school. "Mrs. Toups, I want you to listen to this 1st grader read this material that I was preparing for 3rd graders."

With that she prompted me to read and I did, impressing both teachers. Mrs. Toups then said, "Young Walter, I want you in my class next year." I was, and she was also a wonderful teacher, giving me a great deal of after-hour teaching.

Theresa Broussard taught 3rd grade upstairs, where I joined her class for that year. She was much more rigid and less warm than Miss Madeline or Mrs. Toups, but insisted on excellence in learning.

In the 4th grade, Mrs. Mae dePerrodil, the third sister, became my teacher. She was quite different from her sisters, being quite the disciplinarian. She insisted on attention and didn't tolerate any disturbances, and continued pushing learning and excellence.

She was even known to take out her paddle, while escorting disturbers into the cloak room. It was rare for one to go to the cloak room more than once. The cries emitting, along with the sound of the swatting paddle, made everyone attentive.

There have been many teachers following the three Broussard sisters that have attributed to my education and success in life. Mrs. Lemaire, 5th and 7th Grade, Mrs. Figueson, 6th Grade and Mr. Linscombe, Mrs. Bush and Miss Saltzman in Gueydan High School.

Our high school Band Director was a young, rather immature Mr. Brown, with a strange face. It was pointed upward, with a very prominent nose, and he was nicknamed "Pickles" by his students. I played clarinet, sax and bass drum, and despite "Pickles" short temper, he taught music well. Shortly after our graduation, he married one of my classmates, Laura Lejeune.

The last, and one of the foremost influences on me, was Coach Dorchous, who came to our high school as head coach in 1948, when I was a sophomore. He was a dynamic young man, with a teacher wife. They were from Iowa State and were near foreigners, with their Yankee accent. He was most successful coaching our basketball team to District Title and State Runner-Up. He started up a football team and track team, nonexistent to that point. Our track team placed in District and I went on to run for L.S.U.

Coach moved away shortly after I graduated from high school. I completely lost contact with him until our 20th Class Reunion, where he appeared by someone's invitation. It was an excellent function, reuniting with Coach and many old classmates. There I learned that his wife had died two years earlier, and he was retired and never remarried. Margie, a good friend and old classmate, recently divorced, was also at the reunion. I had thought that it would be nice if she and Coach got together, but there was no evidence of any interest during our time together.

Several weeks after our reunion, I received a call from Coach at my office during a workday. I was most surprised and wondered why the call. Immediately when I answered the phone, Coach apologized for bothering me.

"Walter," he said. "I have been wanting to speak to you ever since we had our get-together, but I was embarrassed and put it off. I hope you will forgive me and hope you can help me. You are aware that my wife died and I have been single for two years. I haven't had any inclination to date until I saw Margie. I know you and she have always been good friends, and I know she is recently divorced. Do you think she would consider dating me for fun, with no serious intent?"

"Coach," I replied, "I believe she would love to date you and I urge you to pursue this, as it will benefit both of you."

After the conversation, I heard nothing further from him, until six months later, when one of my classmates, a resident of Gueydan, informed me that they had wed. Last I heard, they still are, forty years later.

GROWING UP WITH RELIGION

Growing up in the small, prairie, Cajun village of Gueydan, Catholicism was by far the most common religion, with small Baptist and Methodist churches serving those that were not. A very small group of "Holy Rollers" remained, but were largely unknown until they had their revival.

The Catholic Church building was located in the middle of a square block in the center of town and was the largest non-industrial building in the vicinity. It was a Spanish style building resembling the Alamo, with a large bell, whose peals could be heard over the entire town. This sound signaled the parishioners to attend mass every day of the week and twice on Sunday, and what seemed like continuously during Lent.

Father Garneau was the first and only priest, a French Canadian, who came to Gueydan in the early part of the twentieth century. He spoke French, as well as English, and blended well into the Cajun French speaking community. The 6:00 a.m. mass was entirely in French, including the sermon, of course excepting the Latin portion. Gueydan was a well-known duck and goose hunting area, so he had a 4:00 a.m. mass allowing the hunters to fulfill their Catholic obligation before the morning hunt.

Father Garneau was a dedicated, hardworking, but tight fisted individual, who saved every penny the church received. He made a point of announcing all donations made by the farmers at the end of rice harvesting season, by reading out the names and amounts at the masses on Sunday morning: "Joseph Broussard, two sacks of rice, $10.00. Alphonse Guidry, one sack of rice, $5.00", or the affluent "Raymond Zaunbrecher, five sacks of rice, $25.00."

The collection at mass was handled by men carrying handled collection boxes, that they would carry to each aisle and hold it in front of attendees until they made their donation. The collectors then retired to the rear of the church, where they counted the money and placed it in a small sack including the sum of the collection. Then at the end of mass, they carried this to the front of the church, where Father Garneau accepted the sack, announced the amount, and then blessed it.

He had the Ladies Altar Society caring for the inside of the church, but he mowed the yard, rather than pay someone to perform this task. He was almost an icon, seated on a small lawn tractor, wearing his black cassock in the heat of the day.

Father Garneau was also a stern, no-nonsense individual. This was manifested in his daily activities, but mostly by his penances after confession. The mildest, least sinful penance was one "Holy Rosary" and the more sinful proceeded from there.

Then one day, a rumor began flying through the parish. A new priest was coming to help Father Garneau, who was becoming older and a little feeble. In church, the next Sunday, the announcement was made that Father Simon, (not his real name), a young Cajun French priest was being sent to Gueydan.

Father Simon rejuvenated the Catholic community. He was twenty-five years old, a dynamic speaker, full of energy, and a Godsend to the younger parishioners. He was assigned the 10:00 a.m.

mass on Sunday and in a short time, there was standing room only, an unheard of happening. His sermons were so unique and stirring, that even non-Catholics were attracted.

Father Simon was a very gentle, forgiving person, who began everything with a prayer. He was also well known for his penances after confession, being the exact opposite of Father Garneau. His average penance was three "Hail Mary's" and for the most sinful, he added an "Our Father." If you were assessed a rosary, you were hell bound.

His youth and all his other attributes and activities stimulated the younger group, especially the young men. Two of my friends went to Seminary and one became a priest. The Altar Boys became elevated in status and I wished to become one, but with my Methodist father, that was not possible.

Father Simon had the old deserted original wooden church renovated into The Hall. It was used for teaching Catechism, Knights of Columbus meetings, weddings and best of all, a gathering place for Catholic teenagers on Friday nights. The Catholic church had such sway in the community, that Catholic students were excused from public school the last hour on Friday, allowing them to walk across the street to The Hall for an hour of Catechism taught by Father Simon.

On Friday nights, the Hall was opened and teens gathered for playing checkers and cards, eating snacks, socializing and dancing. The evening was started with a prayer, then Father Simon acted as chaperone and socialized with the young ones. Everyone loved him.

With all of this, Father Simon was nearly a saint and could do no wrong, or so everyone believed.

WHEN PRAYER DIDN'T HELP

The town of Gueydan was surrounded by large, deep rice irrigation canals, which skirted the back yards of the poor and black people in the lower section of the village. In the mid-forties of the twentieth century, these people had no running water and depended upon hand pumped water for drinking. The adult males walked out to the canal for bathing, while the females bathed inside of their house in a large wash tub.

There was no swimming pool and what swimming that was done, took place in the large canals with no lifeguards, resulting in many youngsters never learning to swim. Father Simon must have seen this as an opportunity and started a swimming group. It was a male only group, first composed of Altar Boys, then expanding to other young men.

He gave swimming and diving lessons in Lege's Pond, a large excavated pool surrounded by a levee and fed by a large fresh water pump. This resulted in clear, fresh water and was always cool in the pond, which sat isolated in the middle of a rice field. He would load up his car and enlist teens, who had access to vehicles, to load theirs and then he would lead them, driving a mile out of town, parking on the roadside. They would then walk one half mile, across the field, to the pond.

I had heard of this and it sounded like great fun, so I persuaded my mother to allow me to join the group. She dropped me off on the roadside one afternoon, confident that all would be safe with Father Simon caring for us. Wearing my bathing suit and carrying a towel, I walked to the pond. I could hear the laughter and yells, and as I turned with the pond in view, I was shocked by the sight. Everyone was "skinny dipping." They were all nude, including Father Simon, who was sitting on the bank, naked, with two Altar Boys seated on each side of him. I was the only one wearing a bathing suit and as I approached, Father Simon said, "Walter, take off your bathing suit. They are not allowed here."

After some ineffectual arguing, I removed my suit with great embarrassment. I swam and dived with Father Simon and the rest of the guys for a short time, then left early and walked home quite unhappy knowing I couldn't share this experience with any adult. To inform my mother or any adult would have been met with disbelief and disclaim, and shame for lying about Father Simon promoting nudity. I knew I would have to live with the silence and the question of, "Had I sinned and should I pray?" I felt guilty.

Another upsetting incident occurred shortly thereafter, when I was invited to an evening meeting at the Rectory. My neighbor and friend, Robert, who was also an Altar Boy, told me that Father Simon had a social session with them every Wednesday evening and he had asked Robert to invite me along. Robert told me that Father Simon would start with a prayer, then tell them stories and they would play games. He assured me that there was never anything shady or out of line. It sounded like fun and I needed some reassurance, so I went along somewhat fearfully.

Shortly after we arrived and were led in a prayer, Father Simon said, "I want to show you boys something."

With that, he reached into a nearby drawer and withdrew this object and held it before us. With shock and disbelief, I made out this small metal toy of two men positioned for sodomy. As he moved a handle, the act was performed. He then laughed and said, "This is a sin."

Any personal relationship with Father Simon ceased after this. I went away to college and Father Simon became the personal secretary to the Bishop of the Diocese and was transferred to Lafayette. He remained newsworthy and continued to be mentioned in the "Gueydan News," the local weekly newspaper, that I have continued subscribing to this day.

At age forty-five, Father Simon's demise was headlined, with no information as to the cause or circumstances of his death. Through my friends, who still resided in Gueydan, I found out that the word on the street was that, "He had killed himself."

Sometimes prayers don't help.

CAMP MINNEWANCA

Entering high school in the small Cajun agricultural community of Gueydan meant a youngster could now join the FFA, the Future Farmers of America. This was a rite of passage from youngster to young man.

The FFA was a countrywide organization composed of local, district and national chapters. Its purpose was to promote and teach young potential farmers and promote competition and fellowship between the local chapters. It also gave competitive members the opportunities to display their animals and produce at FFA sponsored events. Those predisposed to leadership could run for office in their local or district chapter and, if really eager, the state organization.

I immediately became politically motivated, running for office in the local chapter with the encouragement of our Ag teacher and FFA counselor, Robert Linscombe. In a couple of years I was the local President, District Vice President and State Reporter, the first time someone in our local club had become a state officer.

Being a state officer required attending training sessions in Lafayette and Natchitoches. A meeting of officers from around the state was held and we learned that all officers were encouraged to attend a national training seminar in Michigan, with all expenses paid. Having only traveled to one other state, Texas, this was an opportunity that would never recur. The thought of traveling from a state marking the southern boundary of the U.S. to a state marking the northern boundary, and through all the states to get there, was overwhelming. I signed up immediately, before even asking my parents. When I returned home, I immediately contacted Mr. Linscombe and he reassured my parents of the safety and honor of the trip.

Time drew near for our visit to Camp Minnewanca, on the banks of Lake Michigan. We were all informed of the type of clothing to pack, much of which seemed warm, leaving 90 degree south Louisiana. Five officers and the State Counselor, Mr. Smith, met in Natchitoches and loaded up a station wagon, which even though large and spacious, was packed to the hilt.

Mr. Smith did most of the driving, but was relieved by the two older officers. No one had experienced travel such as this and every time we crossed a state line, we all cheered. After two days and crossing seven states, we arrived at the bank of Lake Michigan and Camp Minnewanca. Immediately we understood the need for warm clothing, with early morning temperatures in the 50's.

We were given instructions, our itinerary and rules. We had four man tents with army cots, blankets, shower and bathroom facilities for every five tents. Every day was to begin with a bugle reveille. We then met on the beach in swimsuits, freezing, performed calisthenics for thirty minutes and on command ran to the water's edge and plunged in. This was an absolute shock to us deep southerners, as the water felt as though it was freezing. After the first day, all of us Louisiana boys decided we would sleep in until the arising activities were over, and we did.

Every day was filled with fun, fellowship and education. We had game contests between tents, canoeing on Lake Michigan and attending lectures. I still remember the most informative speaker. He was an M.D. giving a talk on sex, and I learned what the Rhythm Method was and how to perform it.

Camp Minnewanca was an experience of a lifetime and enhanced the life of a young Cajun boy beginning the travels of life.

I perused the internet (2016) and found Camp Minnewanca still exists.

POOWEE AND OOHWEE

In the prairie Cajun country of South Louisiana, there was an abundance of small wild animals and many of the young people made pets of captured rabbits, raccoons, possums and, yes, even skunks. One of my friends had a pet skunk and I always envied him. Skunks were beautiful animals, black with a white stripe running down their back and black bushy tails. However, their malodorous nature prevented people from being too close to them.

Being a derring-do person, even at an early age, I didn't hide my desire for a pet skunk. Even though the expression of it was met with derision and disbelief from my teenage friends. My father even gave his permission, informing me that I must accomplish it on my own, without his help.

As I turned fourteen, my desire to become a medical doctor and perhaps, a surgeon, became imbedded in my brain and my desires and actions became guided by this. The thought of operating on a baby skunk, removing the musk glands and having a rare pet thereafter as the reward, reinforced my wishes.

With that, I discovered a gentleman in my small town, who was known to be able to deodorize skunk. I learned where he lived, and as telephones were rare in those days, I walked to his house to ask if he would help and instruct me in the procedure if I captured a baby skunk. Mr. Francois readily agreed and advised me to contact the local pharmacist to obtain a surgical knife and the anesthetic agent, Chloroform, in preparation for the procedure. Now all I had to do was capture the skunk.

My friend and one of my Dad's workers, Lou, and I, were helping to build a cattle pen on an earthen ridge near the edge of the marsh. As we had stopped to eat our lunch, I happened to look up and see a mother skunk come out of a burrow nearby, followed by her five babies.

"Look Lou, I would love to have one of those little skunks," I explained. Having heard my desires, Lou was aware of my plans.

"Come on," he said, as he jumped up and ran toward the brood yelling. I followed him as the frightened mother skunk turned back toward the opening of the burrow. "I'll close the opening behind the mother and we will catch the babies," he yelled excitedly.

I followed closely with some fear of being sprayed by the mother skunk. However she went into the hole followed by her litter. Before the last two babies entered, Lou stomped down on the opening, closing it. The two small skunks could not move very fast and were easy to catch and place in a box to carry home. My dream was happening.

Lou and I examined them and found them to be brother and sister. They had a slight skunk odor due to proximity with their mother, but were too immature to produce and expel musk. Nevertheless I named them Poowee and Oohwee.

The pharmacist, to whom I had spoken earlier, had the materials ready when I stopped on my way to Mr. Francois' house.

I had contacted Mr. Francois the evening before, when we arrived home after work. He advised me to feed them milk with a baby doll bottle and nipple, but nothing after midnight. They nursed hungrily on this offering and slept through the night, as I observed them through my insomniac night.

Arriving at Mr. Francois' house, I was filled with excitement, happiness and apprehension. My heart was beating rapidly and the thought of cutting into a living animal would not leave me. Mr. Francois would perform the first surgery on the male, Poowee, while instructing me. Then I would follow on Oohwee.

The anesthesia would be administered by placing a small paper bag, containing cotton balls doused with chloroform, over the skunk's head until it stopped moving, at which point the bag was removed and surgery would progress. When the skunk began to move, the procedure was repeated until the surgery was complete.

With Poowee asleep, Mr. Francois washed his hind legs with soap and water and shaved the upper inner area overlying the musk glands. An iodine solution was swabbed over the area and he incised the skin. I was so intent on observing and learning, that all of the pre-surgical emotions were gone until the procedure was complete and it was my turn.

Oohwee was unconscious under the anesthesia as I prepared the surgical area. As I grasped the scalpel, the reality of what was happening struck me, causing difficulty catching my breath and a marked tremor of my hands. A great feeling of fear and anxiety was overwhelming.

"Just relax and take a deep breath," said Mr. Francois. "You will do everything easily, but you must relax."

Following his instructions, I calmed and opened the skin with no difficulty. The remainder of the procedure went just as well. I was elated as Oohwee began to move and regained consciousness. My first surgery! The emotional high was so great that I knew I wanted to be a surgeon when I grew up.

Poowee and Oohwee recovered uneventfully and lived in a box in the windowed rear room. As they grew, the attempts to use their musk glands continued, as it was genetically ingrained. Squatting on the front paws while spinning around, tail elevated, aiming toward anything that attracted their attention. This continued to frighten our small dog, who had experience with skunks. To humans, they were playful and friendly, but never as close as domesticated dogs or cats.

I remember Poowee and Oohwee with fondness and thankfulness to this day for the lifelong effect they had on me and my life.

PETE'S BARBER SHOP

Saltzman's Barber Shop stood out on the main street of the small Cajun town of Gueydan. With its white and red striped barber pole out front, there was no way to mistake it for the two saloons, one drugstore, two grocery stores and the picture show that composed the remainder of the buildings on the paved eight block boulevard. Besides being the only place to get a gentleman's haircut, it was the center of information shared by men only.

Barber Pete Saltzman was standing behind the only barber chair trimming the hair of Roy Broussard, while T-Bob sat patiently awaiting his turn. They all looked up expectantly as the known town gossip, Joe Boudreaux, walked through the bell ringing front door.

"Good morning, my friends," Joe said as he sat next to T-Bob. "Have you all heard the bad news about Elias Lejuene?"

Roy answered, "Yes, I heard he suddenly dropped dead while at work at the Pure Oil Camp yesterday, probably from a heart attack."

"That's right," said Joe. "But that's only part of the story," and with that he had everyone's attention.

Pete the barber questioned, "What else happened? I was surprised because he was just in here two days ago for a haircut and was looking and feeling fine."

Joe didn't answer for a short time, letting the tension build.

"The word is that his wife, Joyce, had been messing around with Elias' brother for some time. Elias went to work yesterday, but wasn't feeling well. He left work, returning home, unexpectedly catching the two in the act. That's when he had the heart attack and died," Joe finally added.

"I heard several months ago that they were having an affair, but didn't believe it. Elias and Joyce were a loving, happy couple and had been married twenty years. His only brother, Sam is five years younger, was also happily married with two young children," said T-Bob.

About that time Pete completed Roy's haircut and Roy stood and paid Pete his one-dollar charge, saying as he walked out, "I'll see you later, I'm sure we haven't heard the last of this."

T-Bob took his place in the barber chair telling Pete, "Don't cut it too short, I just want a trim." Things were unusually quiet in Saltzman's Barber Shop for a while. Four weeks later, Joe returned for another haircut. The barber shop was empty, a very unusual situation, and Joe immediately sat in the chair.

"I need the top of the line haircut today, Pete. I have a wedding to attend and my wife wants me to look young," said Joe.

"No problem," said Pete, as he draped Joe with the apron.

"Have you heard the latest on Elias' death?" Joe asked.

"No, the last I heard was shortly after his death that the coroner was going to have an autopsy done. Because of that, I thought there were questions about his death."

"Well the autopsy report is back," Joe said in the authoritarian manner he typically used when he had information others didn't have. "They found evidence of cyanide, a poison, in his body."

MAN AGAINST NATURE

Growing up in the Cajun Prairie meant experiencing a closeness to nature from the early days in one's life. Nature was part of the culture as manifested by the names of some of the small Cajun towns, such as Cocodrie, meaning alligator and Carencro, getting its name from Carrion Crow or more commonly Buzzard.

The nearby Bayou de Torture, Bayou Tail of the Turtle, was named by the local folklore, giving the origin of the waterway to a turtle making its way in the swampy area, dragging its tail, leaving a trail for water to wash through over the eons. This in turn made the turtles, snakes, catfish, garfish, raccoons, possums and many other creatures part of the natural habitat.

The lower Cajun Prairie became known for its prolific bird population, attracting hunters from all over the world to harvest the ducks and geese. Bald Eagles, Osprey and multitudes of smaller birds were part of everyday life. The most common large one being the Buzzard, which glided gracefully through the air, searching for dead animals on the ground on which they would feed, preventing the buildup of malodorous, unsightly, decaying flesh.

Unfortunately, when man and nature are intertwined, there are frequently clashes where one or the other is harmed.

My father was a cattle farmer and, as such, was a close steward of the welfare of his herd. He would drive over dirt roads and trails, through the fields, at times finding a cow bogged down in a ditch, unable to move itself out. Then he would get a helper, tie a rope around its head and pull the animal to safety.

One afternoon, he returned home and informed my brother and me that the "damned buzzards" had killed a newborn calf. He had come up on the dead newborn, covered with buzzards, feeding away on the umbilical material, with the mother standing nearby, making frequent forays to frighten the birds away. Daddy was convinced the buzzards had become carnivorous and had killed the calf.

He also became certain this occurred because of an overpopulation and he had to reduce the number of buzzards or lose more newborn calves. To do this, he built a trap of chicken wire and small light wood measuring twelve feet square and four feet high. There was a funnel-like opening on one side, leading into the cage. This opening measured two feet on the outside, sloping down to eight inches inside. He then carried this out into the field, laying it down with the calf in the center as bait.

I asked him, "What is going to keep the birds from coming back out, since the funnel opens in and out?"

He explained to me, "Buzzards look up as they walk around and look down only when feeding. They will look above the small inner opening and will not escape. We will return tomorrow and this pen will be filled with buzzards and we will shoot them all."

The next day we returned and as we approached the trap, we viewed an incredible sight. It was filled with large buzzards, some feeding, some just standing, and others walking around inside with their heads elevated and eyes above the inner funnel opening.

My brother and I stood about fifteen yards away and proceeded to slaughter the encaged buzzards with no remorse, as they had killed one of our newborn livestock. This was quite a gross undertaking, greater than the blood and guts from the shots, mainly because of the manner in which buzzards digest their food, making it available to feed their young. They take in very small particles and digest this quickly into liquid. When feeding their offspring, the mother bird inserts her beak into the hatchlings open mouth and regurgitates the liquid stomach contents, thus nourishing the young bird. In the shooting, the buzzards would recoil off the ground when struck and vomitus would fly from its beak and, if struck in the neck, it would squirt out of that opening also.

We had dressed properly to dispose of the remains with rubber boots, long sleeved coveralls and rubber work gloves. After the shooting was competed, we lifted the cage and moved it a distance away. We then placed some wood in a pile and used pitchforks to pile the buzzards atop it. This was not a pleasant, delicate task. The entire mess was then doused with gasoline and set afire. Following this, there was a noticeable diminishment in the number of buzzards in the vicinity and we lost no more newborn calves.

HONEY

Any time I see the beautiful, clear, golden, thick fragrant syrup or taste honey it brings back pleasant memories of times in my youth when I would assist my father in his beekeeping duties. This was a hobby he had developed into a profitable sideline business, as honey was scarce and brought a good price in the prairie Cajun town of Gueydan.

Beekeeping was not a complex business, but required a knowledge of, and use of, the available natural materials in producing the finished product. Helping my father, I learned about the bee colony composed of the queen, who laid the eggs producing new bees, worker bees who flew from the hives and harvested the nectar from flowering plants, and drones who cared for newborns inside the hives.

Bee swarms also required his attention and were instrumental in replenishing his stock. Swarms were large number of bees accompanying a new queen flying away from the colony to find a new home. The swarm flying together would find a new home, like a hole in a tree or open area in a wall, where they would all light to begin a new colony. When these gatherings were sighted, the neighbors would notify my father, who would then don his protective garments and headgear and approach the swarm, which he would probe until he sighted the queen. He would then pick her out of the swarm and place her into a nearby hive. She would then shortly be followed by worker bees and drones and a new functioning hive would be formed. I recall at one time he had ten hives in different locations, all accessible to robbing.

Robbing the beehives, as harvesting the honey was called, was the premier event of a beekeeper's life and Daddy always required my help. Dressing him in his protective suit and helmet and gloves was most important and even with all of the precautions, he would sometimes be stung. These were always treated as a slight bother unless there were several at once. A hand held smoker, which extruded smoke on the bees, temporarily disabled the bees and kept them away when necessary.

Then he would approach the hive, remove the lid, while smoking the area, reach in with his gloved hand and remove the slats filled with honey, remove the honey, replace with new honeycombs and then close the hive. Depending on the number of hives, this could take several hours including filling a large tub with combs and honey. This then went to Mother, who placed it in jars in preparation for sale, with combs and some without combs after straining. The combs in jars were attractive to people who enjoyed chewing on the honey filled wax.

All of these memories brought back by the mere sight of honey, prompted remembrance of my father's constant need to stay busy. Spare time was always filled with some activity and retirement removed many of those. He no longer had a full time job and loss of cattle farming removed his time spent riding his horse. He replaced that by becoming a homing pigeon enthusiast. This necessitated building a home site, learning about the art of homing pigeons, and the purchasing of several pigeons and getting them acclimated to their new home. Initially he would take two or three pigeons five miles into the countryside, where he would lose them and watch them circle and then fly toward home. He would then return home, awaiting the pigeons' return, when he would feed them. This grew into trips of fifty miles or more from home where they would be released. He would race them back home in his pick-up truck.

The return of these memories produced by the mere sight of honey is accompanied by sadness due to the feeling of loss, but more so by the memories of happiness that accompanied these experiences and the closeness to my father at that time of our lives.

BRONCO BUSTING

Attending rodeos was fun and fashionable when I was in high school. The rodeo riders were admired and envied, but were rare in the everyday world. My Dad was a frequent attendee of rodeos and an admirer of his friend, Elias, who was a bucking bronco rider. Elias owned a small rodeo ring out of town where he practiced and taught his son, Robert, the skills and art of bronco-busting.

I had verbalized to my Dad my wish to participate in the sport, and being enthused with the idea, he encouraged me by arranging a teaching and practice session with Elias at his rodeo ring after school. But he warned me not to tell Mother, as she would veto the project completely out of fear of my being injured.

The day arrived, and I spotted the rodeo ring as we turned off and approached it on a small dirt road. Inside it was Elias and his son, Robert, holding the bucking horse I was to ride. This was my test to see if I could be a bronco-buster, and I was quite apprehensive.

Dad parked his pick-up truck and we walked over to the ring. As we approached, Robert beckoned to me and greeted me with, "Since I am more experienced, I will give you instructions on how to go about bucking bronco riding."

He pointed to a thick rope around the horse's body, behind the front legs, which was tied together on the top between the shoulders.

"This is what you hold to keep from falling, as well as clamping your legs tight to the horse. The halter that I am holding will be removed after placing him into the holding pen behind us," instructed Robert.

The holding pen was a narrow boarded area, slightly taller and longer than the horse. With the horse enclosed in the pen, the rider could climb up the backside and mount astride the bronco. When everything was ready, the front side was swung open, allowing the horse loose to become a bucking bronco.

My heart had been beating rapidly before this explanation and now was racing with pulses felt over my body.

"Are you ready?" asked Robert.

I looked around and noticed Dad and Elias mounted on saddled horses to be used as rescue, if the rider appeared to be falling.

"I guess so," my trembling voice answered.

"Well, mount up," Robert replied as he helped me up the backside and upon the now quiet bronco in the pen.

I grasped the holding rope and pulled myself tightly to the body and nodded to Robert affirmatively as he opened the front gate.

There was a moment of silence and stillness, suddenly broken by the feel of the earth moving under me as the bronco broke out vigorously with a multitude of small jumps on the fore and hind legs, only to be joined by an elevated twisting leap. My only thought and entire effort was to maintain my balance and remain atop the horse.

What appeared to be lengthy minutes, but in reality were only short seconds, passed until I felt myself being separated from the airborne body of the bronco. With my arms outstretched and legs crouched, I struck the earth with a force never before experienced. My next conscious realization was my Dad kneeling next to me, holding my head.

"I'm o.k.," I mumbled, as I attempted to rise.

"Just lay there for a few minutes and then you can get up," said Dad.

Shortly, I arose with little pain and much stiffness. One thing stood out in my mind over all else.

I was not going to be a bronco-buster.

THE BEST DECLAIMER

I was cleaning out the attic recently, when I stumbled upon a treasure. Opening an old cardboard box, I found a very old, velvet covered case which enclosed a gold medal. Excitedly, I looked at it and found it had been awarded to my grandfather, J. W. Daniel, in 1890, a man about whom I knew very little. On the other side of the medal was imprinted "Best Declaimer." This did nothing other than magnify the puzzle, as I had no idea what was a "Best Declaimer."

My grandfather was largely unknown to me and whom I remember seeing only once in my childhood, in 1940. He resided in an old two story boarding house, nearly bedridden, in the small Texas town of Mexia, many miles from Gueydan. I knew nothing of his earlier years and my father never spoke about him. I remember my father leaving to drive to Mexia for his funeral. This lack of knowledge made the medal and its story even more enticing. My brother, Carly, remembered being shown the medal and told by our father that it was bestowed upon his father for being a good speaker. No other family members were available for information due to the demise of all of his siblings. That left the internet for further research.

First, I had to understand, "What was a Declaimer?" Clarification was obtained reading about an award given yearly by Grandbury College, founded in 1877, in Fort Hood County, Texas. Their description was:

> "Best Declaimer – a gold medal and $10.00 will be awarded to The *Best Declaimer* in Freshman and Sophomore classes. A competent committee shall be appointed to decide the question, who will take into consideration Gesticulation, Articulation, Modulation and Pronunciation, etc."

This made it very clear that my grandfather was an intelligent and probably learned man in his young days. I still don't know from where the medal originated, as his name was not on the award list from Granbury College in 1890.

The medal reinforced something I had already learned about my lineage. While applying for a passport at the National Center in New Orleans many years ago, the secretary who was processing the information asked, as she perused my birth certificate, "Do you know that your last name is different from your father's?"

Very puzzled I replied, "No, what are you talking about?"

In answer to which she pushed my birth certificate toward me and said, "Look closely at the last name of your father, and then yours."

I did this and was immediately astonished as my last name was Daniels with an "s", and his was Daniel without an "s", exactly like the Daniel on the medal. It appears that my father changed the family name on me, and as I discovered later, on my brother, Carly, as well.

The reason for this is totally unknown and will probably remain so, but knowing I am the offspring of a "Best Declaimer" is quite gratifying.

I plan to bestow the medal on my grandson, William Daniels, who is the only male grandson carrying the Daniels name and genetic heritage. He is very intelligent and may be a "Best Declaimer".

THE DOCTOR YEARS

***

A GIFT UNFORGOTTEN

As high school graduation approached, I excitedly prepared for college, knowing that applications to L.S.U. would be sent during the early summer months. I knew from early high school that I would go to L.S.U. and made the grades and participated in extracurricular activities to ensure acceptance. It was always known to me, my school mates, teachers, and family that this would happen, so it was quite a surprise when out of the blue one day, my mother asked.

"Do you still plan to go to college?"

"Well, of course. This is a surprising question," I replied.

"Have you spoken to your father about this, and whether he can and whether he will pay for it?" Mother questioned.

"I assumed that was understood long ago and didn't know I needed to approach it again," I replied, staring at her with this questioning look.

"I think it would be courteous, meaningful and respectful for this plan to be laid out so that all concerned understood it fully," Mother stated very forcefully.

A feeling of dread and fear nearly overcame me. My future for as long as I can remember is in jeopardy.

"Well, I will certainly do it, because I don't want to wait to the last minute and end up with no support. I sort of thought all along that you and Daddy had talked about this. Will you help me and talk to him before I do?" I questioned.

"No", she replied. "You are a young man, approaching independence and you must act accordingly," she said, leaving no question as to her feelings.

I was somewhat disappointed and apprehensive at the thought of having to speak directly to my father, asking him for long term help and his dedication to paying for it. He was always very difficult to discuss things with, especially finances. My mother was easy, and subsequently made all of the minor decisions.

In the evenings after his work day, Dad would sit in his easy chair and read his daily newspaper. I took this as an opportunity and sat across the room from him and said, "Daddy, I have something very important to talk about to you."

Putting his paper aside, he sighed, "O.K.".

"As you know, I'm graduating from high school with good grades and want to go to college and then medical school, but I can't without your help in paying for it. That is what I'm asking for."

Without hesitation, he asked, "How much will it cost?"

"I have done some research and it looks like the cost for each semester will be for tuition and secondhand books about $250, room and board $110 a month, and other miscellaneous things like food and clothing, another $200 a month."

Dad had taken his pen out and written all of the costs on a pad which he scanned and then said, "We can take care of that, but you must make good grades."

He then opened a checking account for me in the local Bank of Gueydan and was never late making a deposit.

I didn't own a car, so I chose the cheapest way to travel when I would go to Gueydan for a weekend visit or holiday. I would hitch-hike. Mother bought me a small, leather suitcase and I bought a large head of L.S.U. Tiger sticker, which I placed on each side, nearly covering it. I would choose an intersection where traffic slowed, place my bag facing oncoming traffic, stand behind it and wave my hand, holding my thumb out while trying to get their attention. I became very successful, usually requiring only three or four different hitches to make the entire trip. The suit-case, with "Mike the Tiger" sticker, was the real attention getter and the drivers that picked me up often commented upon it.

My successful four years of undergraduate school were relatively easy, without money worries and the continuing encouragement by my parents. To get financing for medical school, which was much more expensive, I proposed an agreement with my parents. We would keep a record of all the finances they covered through the four years and when I became financially successful, I would repay them.

This came about several years into practicing medicine and I planned a weekend trip to Gueydan to pay off my debt. Under the same circumstances of over eight years earlier, with my father sitting in his easy chair reading his paper, I sat across the room and said, "Daddy, I have become quite successful in my practice and I want to thank you and Mother for all of your help, and repay you for all of the money you have given me."

Without hesitation, he looked into my eyes and replied, "That is not necessary. I have been repaid many times over by your success and we don't need the money."

"But, Daddy, that would be unfair to my brother, Carly, for me to receive this and him not to receive the same," I retorted.

"Don't worry about that. I have helped Carly many times with loans for farming, cars and other things. He doesn't pay back."

I left from my visit, humbled and with a feeling of thankfulness and appreciation that persists to this day, fifty years later.

A LESSON WELL LEARNED

When I stopped by the mailbox at the Fraternity House, I was surprised to see a letter from L.S.U. Medical School. My application for acceptance had been sent early, hoping to get early acceptance and the cessation of worry. Excitedly, I tore open the envelope and pulled out the one-page letter that read, "We, the Board of Supervisors of L.S.U. Medical School, regret to inform you that your application to L.S.U. has been rejected."

No ifs, ands or buts and no reason. Simply "Rejected!" I was shocked and distressed as I had expected acceptance. Granted, my grades were not superior, but I thought well enough. Obviously not.

In pre-med, one can apply at the end of three or four years. I chose to attend summer school and apply at the end of three years to save money.

My high school grades were all excellent without a great deal of study. My first year of pre-med with a moderate amount of study was slightly over 3 points, which was a B. Unfortunately, I began to enjoy the social aspects of college. I joined a fraternity, lived in the Frat House, made the L.S.U. Track Team, which required traveling to other colleges, and indulging in other activities that took the place of study.

The rejection was an eye opener. I suddenly realized that I might not achieve the goal of my life, to be a Medical Doctor. I knew that continued activities in the same vein would prevent success and immediately began to make drastic, but necessary changes. I moved out of the Frat House, scheduled courses easier than Chemistry and Physiology, quit the track team and dedicated four hours a day to outside the classroom study.

The results were as expected, the Dean's List for the next two semesters, meaning an average of B+ or 3.5 grade point average. Then it was time for med school application again. Part of the application required that a professor of your choice would write a letter of recommendation. I chose Doctor Gottleib, the Dean of the Foreign Language Department and the Professor of Germanic Languages. I had completed three semesters of German under him with all A's, so I had a good personal, as well as a scholarly relationship with him. I was certain that he would highly recommend me and that was important.

The application had to be competed and submitted by November and the first return by February. Because of my failure on the first application, I didn't expect to have an early return. The February returns came out and several of my classmates received acceptance. I was not overly concerned by not getting acceptance in the first group.

The next application notification was in April and at that time I found a letter from L.S.U. Medical School in my mailbox on April 5. There was hesitance and fear as I held the letter in my hands before opening it. I knew that in my hands was something that would affect me the remainder of my life. With an anxious tremor, I unfolded the enclosed page and read, "The L.S.U. Board of Supervisors is proud to welcome you to the Freshman

Class of L.S.U. Medical School of 1955. Further directions will follow."

The emotions of happiness, gratitude and relief were near overwhelming, nearly to the point of tears. The knowledge of good decision making and its rewards were obvious and were well learned and would remain with me and stand me in good stead in future endeavors for the remainder of life.

BODY MOVERS

With only a few days of dissection remaining on our wretched cadavers, Jack Stone, a good friend and classmate, and I were called into the office of Dr. Gustav, our anatomy professor at L.S.U. Medical School. We had developed a relationship with him, which was closer than usual between professor and student. He knew that Jack and I were both married with one child, and also were stressed financially and were always looking for a way to earn an extra dollar.

"Would you guys be interested in making twenty bucks on Saturday morning?" he asked.

Well, twenty bucks in 1955 was a lot of money and we jumped at the opportunity before we knew what we would be doing.

"As the first dissection is ended, we'll be removing the used cadavers and replacing them with fresh ones. However, you must be strong of heart and stomach as this will require you doing and seeing things you have never done before," he admonished us. With the thoughts of dollars foremost in our minds, these words meant little.

We then made arrangements to meet him on Saturday morning in the basement of the medical school, an area we didn't know existed. That morning, dressed in old work clothes that would be discarded, we entered the school building and walked down a flight of stairs where Dr. Gustav greeted us and led us into a large dreary room, empty other than two large trailer-like gurneys and a large circular crank on the wall opposite the door. The center of the room was made up of a vat, about twenty-five feet square, covered with hinged doors joined in the center.

As he had been instructed, Jack turned the large crank and the doors opened, releasing an almost overpowering smell of the formaldehyde-filled vat. Dr. Gustav switched on the lights in the vat allowing us to view the inner area. We were bewildered as we realized the contents of the vat was composed of nude bodies, floating face down in the formaldehyde. Each had a rope harness circling the upper arms and shoulders, and then joining in the posterior thorax.

Then we noted a more horrific thing than we had dreamed of seeing. Hanging on the walls, suspended by hooks and bobbing in the formaldehyde, were a multitude of infants, all preserved. The child cadavers were aged from newborn to two to four years old, the ages of our sons. We both had to sit for a few minutes to allow ourselves to accommodate to this unbelievable spectacle.

Dr. Gustav then handed us an eight-foot long aluminum pole, shaped like a shepherd's crook. With this, we proceeded to hook a floating cadaver, pull it to the side and then together, lift it out of the vat and into the trailer-like gurney. We repeated this until we had them stacked four deep. Needless to say, after a short time, we were stinking and wet.

After loading one gurney, we took the elevator to the dissecting room on the sixth floor. There we removed the used bodies off four dissecting tables and placed them in the empty trailer gurney we had brought along. We placed the fresh cadavers on the now empty tables. We then returned to the vat room, taking the gurney containing the used bodies along with us. These would be disposed of by the city sanitation department. We repeated this until the job was completed, after about four hours. We were then paid our twenty-dollars and offered a much needed shower and clean scrubs to wear home.

In our first dissection, Jack and I learned that the condition of the cadaver had a strong influence on a successful endeavor. While moving the bodies, we had noted two cadavers that were in obviously better condition than any of the others. They were younger and without obvious body defects. We had decided to approach Dr. Gustav about us getting one of these good bodies for our dissection, as a bonus for all of our hard work. As we asked him, he smiled and said, "Gentlemen, you certainly know that I can't do anything that would give one student an advantage over another. I am afraid I must turn down your request, but out of curiosity, which cadaver would you chose?" We pointed out the young female.

Monday the entire class gathered in our large classroom to select cadavers for the next dissection. Dr. Gustav stood at the head of the room with the capless skull holding numbered slips in his hand. I was chosen to select the number for our group and decided to get into the end of the line. As I followed, I noted each student ahead of me reaching up and pulling a numbered slip out of the skull. As I got closer, I could see into the skull and noted when the student ahead of me picked his number, it was empty. Dr. Gustav then loosened his grip, moving his thumb, allowing a white slip to fall into the empty skull. I picked up that slip, looking into Dr. Gustav's smiling face, strongly suspecting our body choice would be favorable. The young lady cadaver was ours and for the remainder of the semester, our dissection went well.

DEATH AND DOCTORS

People going into Medicine know that they will have to deal with the inevitable, Death, even though their goal will be a long, healthy life for their patients. Doctors' duties require their attendance at end of life events and continue for short times after.

I knew at an early age that I wanted to be a doctor, and the doctor in the small Cajun town of Gueydan took every opportunity to encourage me. When my mother's sister, Aunt Elite, developed breast cancer and had to have a mastectomy, they invited me to view the procedure as the first operation I had ever seen. She survived the operation, but I had my first close death experience when she expired six months later.

My first medical death experience was in my third year of medical school, when I was assigned a patient, Joe, on the medical ward of Charity Hospital. Joe had a terminal illness and I knew of the illness and its medical ramifications, but had little knowledge or experience to use in dealing with this during my everyday relationship with Joe. Fortunately, my professor, Dr. Berman, took me aside for instructions.

"Walter, how do you feel about Joe having an illness with no chance of survival?"

"Dr. Berman," I replied, "It makes me feel very sad and I can't talk to him about it."

"It's acceptable to feel sad," replied Dr. Berman, "but you must never allow those feelings to influence the manner in which you deal with Joe medically. You will have many occasions in the future where similar situations may occur. Emotional feelings may cause you to respond in an emotional manner, interfering with independent medical decisions. We must face death as a natural, inevitable happening, even though the happening is unexpected or occurs to someone to whom we are close. This is the reason we are cautioned on treating close relatives."

This was tested several years later during my internship. I was in charge of a ward at the Charity Hospital in Shreveport, The Confederate Memorial Medical Center. My supervisor was a third year Internal Medicine resident, Roger Smith. Roger informed me of the admission to ICU of a twenty-five-year-old man, on life support and comatose from injuries sustained in a motor vehicle accident. This young man, Jim, had been intubated to allow him to breathe temporarily, even though his injuries were so severe that he was expected to die within the next three days. After two days, the situation was unchanged.

Jim's family presented a DNR that Jim had signed a year prior to the catastrophe. DNR means "Do Not Resuscitate," and is a legal document that instructs doctors not to attempt to revive a patient who is in imminent danger of death and not survivable. One week later, with all systems continuing to shut down, a committee of three doctors evaluated Jim and found his state terminal, and the ventilator was discontinued as per Jim and his family's wishes, allowing him to die.

I then encountered an after-death doctor duty, when I was presented with the Death Certificate for my signature. The time of death and cause of death must be certified by a doctor before the body can be disposed of in any way.

Over my career, I have completed and signed many death certificates, but was totally unprepared when at my mother's funeral in Gueydan, the funeral director approached me and asked me to step into the director's office.

"Dr. Daniels, as you know, we do not have a doctor in Gueydan and we need one to sign the death certificate of your mother. I know this is an unusual request, but if you would sign your mother's certificate, it would prevent us from having to transport her body to be viewed by Dr. Abshire in Kaplan, who we use in these situations."

With little emotion, I agreed and completed my mother's death certificate with my signature.

Another situation a doctor encounters is after-death duties, such as when there is no knowledge of why, when or where the death occurred, and especially if there is some suspicion that the patient did not die of natural causes, or might have been killed.

In my career, I have had patients die when I couldn't complete the Death Certificate, as information verifying how, when, where or why the death occurred was not available, or there is some evidence that murder might have occurred. In those situations, I could contact the Coroner, inform him of the situation and get directions as to what to do. Frequently, an autopsy would be ordered. An autopsy is performed by a trained pathologist and can range from a total body examination by dissection, x-rays or laboratory examinations of blood or other body excretions or parts. Under those circumstances the coroner usually signs the death certificate, or unusually, the coroner will give the results of his autopsy to the patient's doctor and request him to sign it.

One of the most difficult and painful death duties is informing family of the occurrence of death. I have performed this onerous task many times in hospitalized or emergency room patients. In these patients, the doctor and nurses are working on the patient in areas closed from the family. When attempts to save or resuscitate the patient are unsuccessful and the patient dies, the attending physician must meet with the family and inform them of the death. Tears, cries and many forms of grief are expressed.

Caring for the many problems of patients is difficult and trying, but the task of dealing with death is one of the most difficult.

SEE ONE, DO ONE, TEACH

Becoming and being a doctor is never related to one person other than one's self. Through the prolonged years of training and exposure to many teachers, the development of a practice depends mainly on one's self. The Practice, a name for the physical and medical area in which one works, is peculiar in that one never completes training, only continues to practice. No matter how long or how much one performs medical tasks, it is always a practice and one continues to practice, never completing it.

In the early days of training, learning is attained from exposure to new procedures, new ideas and new knowledge. This is gained through a multitude of professors, as well as fellow students.

Becoming a Doctor, and getting a medical education, is a team effort from the very first day, when six or eight students join together to dissect a cadaver. From that point on, the education is obtained in small groups up to classes of over one hundred. Individual professors teach these and rarely, if ever, one on one. Students learn something and pass it on to their mates, hence the motto, "See one, do one, teach." This continues throughout one's medical life. Cooperation is built into the system and continues to benefit the most important person, the patient.

Occasionally, an isolated incident will consolidate multiple bits of learning acquired up to that time, and focus to the end point of treatment and cure of the problem.

This was forced upon me in my younger days when I developed a very painful anal swelling. Just a slight touch to the area was extremely painful. I diagnosed a thrombosed external hemorrhoid, which in plain English is a hemorrhoid vein in the anus that has developed a clot blockage, causing it to swell, create great pain and at worst, burst. I knew the treatment was to I & D (incision and drainage), but I didn't know how to do it, especially to myself.

I consulted my associate, friend and surgeon, Dr. Chick Cheramie. "Let's go into the treatment room where you can drop your pants and let me look at this," Chick said. He checked it out and told me, "I'll get the nurse in here, localize the area, open it up, drain out the clotted blood, and it will not hurt anymore, and will heal." After the nurse gathered the tools, local anesthetic and other materials, Chick placed me in the crouched position and described each step of the operation, which was shortly and relatively painlessly completed.

Bandages were applied and Chick said, "That was your treatment and lesson on how to handle a thrombosed external hemorrhoid, if a patient presents with one."

I have performed this numerous times over the years in my practice. It incorporates the knowledge and study of anatomy, physiology, surgery, anesthesiology and multiple teachers. It also allowed me to "see one, do one and teach" or rather, "feel one, do one and teach."

NOT MY PATIENT

A mother brought her eight-year-old child in with an ear ache. Accompanying them was the four-year-old sister, Mary, who was very alert and attentive.

As I examined the older sister, Mary sidled next to me and closely observed me as I examined her sister. I completed the exam, wrote the prescription and instructed the mother and daughter, with Mary placing herself in the middle. Noting this I thought I would involve her.

Grasping my stethoscope, I approached Mary and asked, "Would you like for me to examine you also?"

Mary gathered herself upright, looked at me very forcefully and replied, "No thank you, I have my own doctor."

IT MIGHT HELP

I had completed seeing my last patient, the staff was leaving after preparing for tomorrow and I sat at my desk to finish some must-do paperwork. I then picked up my black bag and walked down the hall toward the partially glassed-in rear exit door.

As I approached the door I perceived a small, shadowy figure near the outside doorway. This immediately produced some apprehension as there recently had been some burglaries by gun carrying thieves. The figure by the doorway appeared to be holding something in his hand, behind his back. I veered into an office with a window overlooking the area and immediately recognized little Bobby, a young patient of mine, whose family lived one half block away.

I returned to the hallway and opened the back door.

"Bobby, what are you doing here and what are you holding behind you?"

"Dr. D." answered Bobby, "I have been wanting to talk to you for a long time and after reading something in the paper yesterday, I thought this would be a good time."

I replied, "Bobby I am through working for the day but you can have a few minutes of my time."

Bobby said, "Dr. D, you have always been my doctor and I like you very much, but I really don't like to go to your office, even if I don't get a shot. The article I read in the paper appeared to help solve the problem and I have brought you a present Dr. D."

With that he removed his hand from behind him and handed me this beautiful, red apple.

"The article said, an apple a day will keep the doctor away. Do you think this will work?"

RESURRECTION OR RAISE ERECTION

In my early days as a Doctor, I had visits by men employed by Pharmaceutical companies who would tout me on the benefits of their company's products and how it excelled above similar products made by other companies. We called them "Drug Reps" and they frequently had small gifts such as ball point pens, pen lights, tongue blades or similar minor inexpensive things with their products' name on it.

One day, John came in to extoll the virtues of his cholesterol lowering medicine. As usual, they would try to get friendly by striking up a conversation that was non-medical. He knew I was an LSU graduate and a staunch supporter of LSU football. In our conversation I told him that I had witnessed the most famous play conversion in LSU history, when Billy Cannon made his game winning touchdown against Ole Miss. He then made his sales pitch and left.

Several days later my receptionist, Debbie, came to the treatment area and informed me, "Drug rep John is up front and he wants to see you."

I was, as usual, overwhelmed, behind and in no mood for interruptions. "Tell him that I just saw him a few days ago and I don't have time for him today," I said.

Debbie departed, only to return a few minutes later saying, "John has a present for you and he will only take a minute of your time."

"O.K., get him in and out quickly."

A short time later, I walked out of the treatment room only to meet John in the hall, holding a new white and gold football which he handed to me. Looking at it I noticed written across it was, "Greetings Dr. Daniels, Billy Cannon #20."

I was astounded and looking at John in disbelief I asked, "Is this real? Did Billy Cannon really sign this?"

He assured me of its authenticity. Stunned, I thanked him and placed the football in a place of honor in my house.

To you who do not understand the importance of this to me, it would be like someone giving you an original copy of the Louisiana Purchase. Billy Cannon remains today an iconic hero of LSU athletics and this gift is something many people would envy greatly. For years, this was the best gift I ever received.

Until one day, when my long standing, treasured receptionist, Debbie, came into my office and informed me, "There is a very unusual drug rep to see you today."

"What do you mean?" I asked.

"I'm not going to tell you, this one will be a big surprise."

A short while later, I returned to my office and seated in it was this beautiful, sexy, young lady with the prescribed accoutrements to attract a male physician's attention: short dress, great legs, big breasts and personable presentation. I had heard of female drug reps but this was my first encounter.

Sally introduced herself and very professionally informed me of her credentials and of her product, Viagra. This male erection enhancing drug had only recently hit the market and this was my first presentation. Sally explained all about the medication, emphasizing its ability to raise erections to the gold standard.

As all of this was transpiring, I thought of the strangeness of this situation. First, here was this very attractive young lady performing as a drug rep, an occupation here-to-fore restricted to men. But ever more unusual was her topic and the manner in which she dealt with male erectile dysfunction. Perhaps in my younger days, I may have been a bit embarrassed but now I was just shocked.

As she completed her pitch, she added, "There is just one more thing. I have a gift for you that I hope will help you remember my product and me."

With that said she withdrew from her pocket a cylindrical object resembling a ball point pen. As she presented the pen to me, she squeezed it and from the center arose this erect portion of the pen.

I thought, "Resurrection or Raise Erection?"

THE HEART MATTERS

Leading with your heart or being open-hearted is difficult for a doctor. From the early days of training, one is met by emotional encounters that tug at one's heart and one learns very early that difficult decisions cannot be based on emotions, but rather on intellect, learning and brain power. Because of this learning and application, doctors frequently come across as being hardhearted, when what is transpiring is heart protection, by placing emotional guards to protect one's self from the damage that would be done by experiencing the emotional turmoil of having to deliver a message of approaching doom to a patient. Despite all of the heart guards, caring for a good friend or treasured family member is fraught with pitfalls, if that person develops a critical illness.

Non-medical encounters occur to everyone and pull at our heart strings. Once, when traveling in China, walking the streets of Beijing, I saw an infant, all alone, kneeling alongside the walkway. She was begging for money to be placed in her cup. Immediately I knew this had to be set up by an adult and thoughts of the hardship of present and future life for this poor child caused the heart to weep. It was impossible not to make a donation even knowing that would only promote the situation. My heart did weep as I placed coins in her cup and she looked up at me with those big brown eyes.

One of a doctor's duties is to allow, listen and care as his patient empties their heart of the struggles, trauma and fear that are causing pain as they are layered time after time until the stress is too great. To have a person trained and caring, accept your heart-breaking tales is healing and comforting.

IN THE OFFICE

Much of a family doctor's career is spent in the office with the infrequent and surprising occurrence of bizarre events.

The Tattoo

My practice required that I perform frequent pre-employment physicals which occasionally produced surprises. On one such occasion, I entered the exam room and there seated wearing a t-shirt and trousers was a non-descript appearing thirty-year-old. As I approached him to do his head and neck exam I noted a tattooed serpent's tail protruding from his shirt collar on his neck.

"Remove your shirt," I ordered as I proceeded to examine his chest. I immediately noted the serpent's body traversed around his thorax and disappeared into the front of his shorts. Mystified by this I was anxious to see the remainder of this art.

Continuing the physical exam, I ordered, "Drop your shorts," and he slowly fumbled, embarrassedly dropping his shorts. Then I viewed the serpent return to the front with the head of the tattoo covering the head of the penis, with its mouth closed.

It was not smiling at my nurse.

Zipped

It was a typical hot summer day with my air conditioned office cool so I was nearly shocked when I entered the treatment room and seated was a young man with an attractive young lady standing next to him. The surprising thing was despite the temperature, the young man was wrapped in a heavy overcoat.

"Well, what's the problem?" I asked, thinking he was trying to stay warm due to chills and a fever.

Obviously ill at ease he replied, "My girlfriend and I were in her living room indulging in a little love play, when her parents drove into the garage as they returned from the movie. I immediately reached down to zip up and this happened."

As he explained, he opened the overcoat and hanging from the half zipped pants was his zipped penis foreskin. After a full explanation I localized the impinged area and unzipped it.

The young man and girlfriend were gratified but never volunteered what they told the parents.

Never Before

Applicants for pre-employment exams are usually quite polite and follow instructions until sex rears its ugly head.

The huge middle aged man awaiting his physical exam appeared slightly obese. I told him to drop his pants for his hernia exam. As I gave him the instructions he gave me this obstinate look and said, "You can't look there."

Puzzled with this, I replied, "If I can't look and examine you then I can't pass you on for your physical exam and you will not get a job and if you continue to refuse, you can leave."

With that he arose and left the office. I returned to my routine. An hour later, Robin, who was working in the reception area, informed me that the man who refused the physical was now back and would allow completion of the exam.

"Put him in an exam room and I will get to him shortly," I ordered. A short time later I entered the exam room where the applicant was seated.

"Stand and drop your pants," I said. Obligingly he responded and I was placed in plain view of a man without a penis. Closer exam revealed flaps of skin and a cavity where his artificial vulva and vagina were now in place. It was my first encounter with a pre-employment applicant who had a sex change operation and passed his physical.

My Bootie

My day had been quite busy and I was running behind, so I was a little upset when this twenty-year-old, African American female gave me her chief complaint.

"I want some more bootie," she said. Thinking I had not understood correctly, I asked her to repeat.

"My bootie is too little and I'm not sexy enough so I want you to give me a shot so that my bootie is larger and attracts more attention," she replied.

Looking at her professionally I knew her complaint and wishes were not attainable and attempted to explain this to her and instructed her on increased food intake and exercise.

I accommodated her wish for surgical reference and never saw her again.

I AM, A GOOD DEED, LONG FORGOTTEN

I Am fortunate. Elderly and healthy, I continue to be loving and loveable. A good life, good genes and good decisions have brought me through eight decades and many trials and tribulations.

I Am an optimist. I always try to see the best in all situations. Good things will happen with a little help and a bright outlook. This quality has enabled me to be successful in my life's work.

I Am a father, step-father, grandfather and great-grandfather. My great-grandson, Kolston is the child of my first grandchild and granddaughter, Lauren and signifies a milestone in my life. He will continue to carry my genetic material and, hopefully, will become a great-grandfather.

I Am a husband. I am blessed with a beautiful, supportive, competent, loving wife of almost forty years, who is my best friend and companion.

I Am an employer. I am very fortunate to have a staff of many years. My office manager has been working for me for thirty-five years and others, twenty-five, fifteen down to two years. Our relationship is more like family than employer/employee.

In my profession, I wear the white coat, which brings with it respect, good compensation, and the ability to heal and keep my fellow man in a knowledgeable, generous and trustworthy manner. Having delivered over one thousand, two hundred babies and caring for family members of the fourth generation, I am truly blessed. I Am a DOCTOR.

Being a Family Doctor of fifty years, it is not unusual to have occurrences that relate to experiences of many years ago, memories of which are frequently gone. One day my office manager, Ana, presented me with a very unique one, when she informed me that a representative of the Louisiana State Prison Authority wished to speak to me about a family that I had cared for and a child I had delivered in the late 60's or early 70's. Ana had searched our medical record file and had no records belonging to Sam and Ida Bonin (not real names). Despite having no records dating back that far, they still requested a personal interview, which I advised Ana to schedule.

For the deposition, I entered the office and was greeted by a personable, young lady with a strong English accent. Upon questioning, she informed me that she was from London and had moved to the U.S. six years ago, and had worked for the Louisiana State Prison Authority division, which represented prisoners who couldn't afford to pay for legal aid. My information was needed to aid in their efforts to get a young man off of death row, supposedly the person I had delivered over thirty-five years ago. How my testimony and information would help, she couldn't tell me.

The entire interview was, "I don't know," or "I don't remember." She showed me pictures of Sam and Ida, and the young man, Jack, that were taken at the time of his birth and scattered years later, none of which I recognized. She then showed me a picture of a rather ramshackle, small house, where the Bonins lived after Jack's birth. To help stimulate my memory, she informed me that I had made a house call shortly after the birth to check on baby

Jack. There was no fan or cooling system in the old house, and the day after my visit I purchased a window air conditioner and had it delivered and installed. That I don't remember either, but it was gratifying to hear of a kind act I performed many years ago.

REMEMBERING LIFE

The ultimate importance to every physician is life. There are many side issues along the way, to which we administer our healing skills that make life happier and more comfortable. The loss of life is the greatest loss and the saving of life is the most rewarding. These together make suicide the most grievous and this manner of dying the most fearsome to physicians.

As a young physician in my early days of practice, I well remember my first case of suicide. I had cared for Sara for the usual problems of teen years and now she was entering the early years of womanhood. Her illnesses were never of a psychological nature, making the happening during the on-call duty in the Emergency room even more difficult and memorable.

The initial sign of an impending crisis was the call from the emergency ambulance. "This is Acadian Ambulance. We are making our way to the hospital with a young lady critically injured with a gunshot wound to the head, apparently self-inflicted. Be there in three to four minutes."

This stimulated the E.R. personnel into high-speed preparation for the arrival of the ambulance and the patient being rolled into the E.R. on the wheeled gurney. The nurses immediately started an IV and C.P.R as I examined the patient and immediately recognized Sara as my patient and pronounced her to be dead. Her wound was horrendous with a shattering opening in the right temporal area, obviously from a bullet wound most likely self-inflicted. Immediately, I realized there was nothing we could do to resuscitate Sara and I ordered everyone to step aside.

The head nurse approached me and advised that some family members had arrived and were waiting outside of the E.R. where she led me. Our presence was greeted by the family members with tears and cries as I verified Sara's death. Then they in turn informed me that she had expressed suicidal thoughts and wishes a few days prior to the incident, but no one took her seriously as she was always happy and had exhibited this other behavior for a very short time.

I completed my E.R. time, which was very busy and prevented my dwelling on the happenings. When I arrived home after work I was overwhelmed with thoughts and questions.

"What caused her to do this? Is there anything I could have done to prevent it? Did she ever show any evidence of depression or suicidal ideation on previous visits?" I questioned myself with personal thoughts of what I could or should have done to prevent this. Sadness and guilt were both prevalent. I was driven to remember, "We need never to be ashamed of tears" and as time passes, "Memories warm your heart from the inside." But they also tear you apart.

WE WERE GIVEN AN ANGEL

All grandchildren are a wonderful gift and are greatly loved by their grandparents, but some are very special even though the grandparents may have many others.

In 1996 I received a call from my son, Bill, telling me that his wife, Kathy, was carrying a grandchild that was special in a way that we didn't wish. They had just returned from getting an ultrasound of their first trimester fetus to determine the sex. However, the ultrasound made the doctor suspicious that this might be a Down syndrome child. A blood test in the next trimester would later confirm the diagnosis. My son was quite upset and asked for my opinion on options as to what they could do. I immediately knew there wasn't a pleasant answer and told him, "Son, there are only two things you can do. The first is to go through the pregnancy in a normal way or number two, Kathy can have an abortion if the blood test confirmation is positive."

The second option was not a consideration and Bill quickly informed me of that. "We will go through this pregnancy and will have a child that we love, even if she has Down syndrome, but tell me what we can expect," he asked.

I replied, "Down's is a genetic defect, the cause of which is unknown. We all have 46 chromosomes, while Down's people have 47. This causes distinct physical characteristics of a flat face and short neck. They also have intellectual disability, usually moderate, in the form of low average intelligence. This is usually mild, but they frequently have physical defects also." (Our granddaughter, Kirsten had heart surgery at nine months and aortic surgery at eleven months.)

With wonderful, loving care by very caring parents, Kirsten has grown into a surprisingly personable young lady. Schooling has also contributed to her development. She attended a private Christian school until the third grade. Since then she has attended public school with special attention to children with disabilities. Several other children with various disabilities attend classes overseen by one teacher and aides. Twice a week she meets with a speech therapist and has special physical education classes.

The result of all of this is a loving, very innocent young lady. She never speaks or thinks badly of anyone, even if she has been treated poorly. She is easily entertained, loves to read and tells her parents about her readings. She picks up personality from T.V. and as a teenager she was a fan of Hannah Montana, singing the songs and doing the dances. From the birth of a child with a future clouded by adversity, we have truly been given an angel. This is exemplified by the way she handled menarche. When she was beginning to have periods, she just took it all in stride and called Kotex, "Grotex."

Her life has also been greatly influenced by her near genius, younger brother, William, who is a straight A student. His intelligence was easily noted in his letters and in statements similar to that made to his father once as they were driving to school listening to the radio.

"Dad, this country is going to the dogs. I don't know what it will be like when I grow up, but it won't be good."

We have been truly blessed with two angels.

THINGS CHANGE

My primary goal when I became a doctor was to help people, especially in medical needs. I had no doubt that I could do this with all the knowledge that I had obtained. Little did I know in those early years, how things would change during my medical career.

Cost of care is much greater today, especially with the increasing appearance of the technical aspects of evaluation and treatment. A chest x-ray and a CBC, a single blood test were the usual things used in making a diagnosis in the early days. Today having a CT scan, angiogram or invasive scans are common. A simple office visit early on was $3 to $5. Near the end of my fifty-three years practicing, it was up to $100 or more.

I began family practice delivering babies and it was common for a family doctor to do this as well as Cesarean or C-sections. I estimate I delivered over one thousand babies. Fifty years later it has become nearly unheard of for a Family M.D. to deliver babies and too expensive with yearly malpractice insurance alone costing $75,000-$200,000. However, Obstetrics was gratifying and formed bonds between me, my patients and their families that have lasted a lifetime.

Being a country doctor in the wetlands of Louisiana presented me with opportunities and obligations unheard of today. The swamp and marshland was filled with wildlife and with the young trappers, fishermen, and hunters that lived there harvesting the bounty. Their medical care was scanty and usually obtained by making their way to the hospital or a doctor's office. Rarely did the doctor make a house call to the trapper's camp and then only in a dire emergency. Childbirth was one of those. A story told to me about Old Doc Gardner of Gueydan, La.:

The young trapper showed up at the doctor's house and informed him that his wife had gone into premature hard labor and could not make it to the hospital. He asked, "Doc would you please come with me and deliver the baby?" With little choice the doc agreed and accompanied the trapper to his pirogue at the edge of the swamp, and then in the boat through the swamps to the trapper's camp. The sound of a wailing newborn filled the air and the Doc and the trapper knew they were too late. Entering the camp, the Doc found it to be spotless with the mother laying in a well-made bed with the freshly washed baby in her arms with the placenta delivered and cord ligated.

These findings shocked the Doc and he asked the mother, "Why did you clean the camp and yourself and baby so well?"

"Well I knew the doctor was coming and I wanted everything to look nice," she said.

Delivering medical care gratis has been part of my practice since I first began. It was always known and continues to be today that some people are impoverished and cannot afford the treatment. Caring for these people at "no charge" has always been an option that I have used. My approaching retirement was hastened by one of the rules imposed upon doctors by "Obamacare." If I choose not to charge a poor patient that I feel cannot afford my care, I must charge them. If I do not, then everyone must be treated for free.

My retirement has brought with it many rewards and some sadness, as well as expressions of appreciation, traversing five generations. This was exemplified by my patient Steve, who said to me, "You are the only doctor that I ever had and I don't know what I will do without you. You saw my butt before anyone else in this world and you helped me handle the death of my mother and father. I have ensured that I see you as long as I can by making an appointment one last time in the last fifteen minutes on your retirement day."

And he did.

YOU DON'T KNOW WHAT YOU HAVE UNTIL YOU DON'T HAVE IT ANYMORE

(Written while approaching retirement)

This title really didn't mean anything until the reality of impending retirement descended upon me. After fifty-five years of living and breathing the full time practice of medicine, that part of my life is about to cease with retirement.

The reality and nearness of it brought to me regularly when my patients of many years approach me with, "You can't quit. You brought me into this world and I have never had another doctor."

Or another patient, with tears in her eyes says, "Are you really going to stop practicing? I don't know what I will do. You have been the doctor for me and my family forever."

These encounters add a real emotional aspect to the big event.

The thought of not seeing my office staff daily is very heartbreaking. They are like family to me with four of them having worked for me from fifteen to forty years. I have shared trials and tribulations, happiness and sadness, good and bad times, births and deaths and simple affection and closeness with each of them.

The loss of this closeness will be difficult to accommodate for all of us.

Retirement will bring a large gap in time, filling activities that henceforth have been occupied by the demands and responsibilities of medical practice. My participation in the Life Writing class will help close the large area which would otherwise be filled with complete boredom. My long time desire to write a novel has become a strong possibility with the knowledge and impetus gained from this class, as well as the examples of the classmates and instructor. This, as well as the encouragement of several of my medical colleagues and my wife, has greatly diminished the feeling of impossibility that has prevented my attempts over many years. Writing will occupy physical and mental free time.

This life-shaking occurrence has also brought out front a reality that we tend to avoid and shovel into the background – Aging. Getting to the age where we have contributed enough years of work that we no longer have to, also indicates that our body has aged that number of years and we are that much closer to the magic final number. With retirement occurring, we can no longer avoid facing the reality that aging is and has occurred. This has a positive note also, as it strongly urges older people to see their doctor and have their health status evaluated.

Things in life that previously were given little precedence, now appear much more important and will get much more attention. I now understand "You don't know what you have, until you don't have it anymore."

THE LOVE OF MY LIFE

***

LOVE COMES IN DIFFERENT FLAVORS

We have all experienced love, but rarely do we analyze the different types of love and how our life handles it. Our love relation with our mate is probably the most common. This type of love has different lengths and occurs at different times of life. The love of mating frequently produces offspring, which are in turn another form of love between child and parent that usually lasts a lifetime and the child mates later in life and has children that renew and present the love of grand parenting. This cycle continues to recur over generations forever.

Human love is not confined to humans and is commonly shared with animals that we call pets. We treat them like dependent humans and lovingly care for them by giving them names, speaking to them and assure their wellbeing with food and shelter.

Dogs are most likely the most common animal that humans love and of course dogs and other animals mate, love animals of their own species and produce offspring. Our love for dogs causes us to speak to them and their understanding vocabulary has been measured up to four hundred words. They of course, cannot speak, but their responses to our words produce signs and symptoms of love by snuggling, rubbing, licking, barking or whining.

The different types of dogs also appear to exhibit their love by the limits of their size. A Great Dane will love his human partner but not in the cuddle fashion of a small Mexican Chihuahua.

Love has been eternal with signs of it going back to the earliest man. Only recently an archaeological finding of a young man and woman, estimated in their twenties were excavated hugging each other. The finding dated back more than five hundred thousand years ago.

Literary authors of poems and books have written about love as long as those have been written.

"None of those other things make a difference. Love is the strongest thing in the world, you know. Nothing can touch it. Nothing comes close. If we love each other, we're safe from it all. Love is the biggest thing there is." David Guterson, 1994, "Snow Falling on Cedars"

"It doesn't matter who you are or what you look like, so long as somebody loves you." Roald Dahl, 1983, "The Witches"

TRUE LOVE IS FOREVER

(A love letter)

Dear Pam,

I never dreamed I would love you many years ago when we first met, it was love at first sight. Initially it was all physical attraction. You were so very attractive, with your beautiful face, glowing skin and great body, that it was love at first sight, when your personality and character peeked around the door. I was immediately aware of many pleasures to come, as I felt your love responding. Unbelievably, this has grown and become more enduring over the years and continues to grow today.

Your inner beauty has always shown through because of your optimism, confidence and love. This has in turn bolstered these features in me and thusly, in our relationship. Because of this, our life has been filled with love and adventure that we have shared with each other alone. The trip down the Grand Canyon, the trips to Europe, Asia,

China, Japan, Russia and the trip on the Concorde were all because of love and have left us many wonderful memories. Your companionship then is not overshadowed by that of our early days together. Early on you were my best hunting partner and fishing buddy, even though you were not happy if you didn't catch the biggest fish.

The days ahead, I'm certain, will continue to be filled with joy and happiness, regardless of adversity, as our love continues forever.

My most precious, darling wife, my love for you will be forever and I thank you for being here for me.

Love,

Your loving husband, Walt

IT WAS JUST A ROUTINE VISIT

That day forty years ago didn't appear to be a world changer at the time, but I couldn't foresee the future at that time either. I remember walking into the treatment room and sitting there was this stunningly beautiful, sexy lady who looked unhappy and was seeking my help to remedy that situation. She immediately volunteered that she and her second husband had separated and she was working to help support her three children. I attempted to be professional in my manner, but I felt empathy and a closeness as I had just completed a similar situation in a divorce.

I completed the office visit by offering some professional advice and prescribing a mild tranquilizer to help allay her severe anxiety. She was instructed to return for follow up in one week.

She returned then and I found her to be much improved and she admitted to feeling more sociable and interested in becoming more friendly and developing dating relationships with male acquaintances. Even as a standoff professional this stirred some interest and questions as to whether I should pursue this. Those thoughts progressed and the slightly questionable ethics of a doctor dating a patient or having a more than cordial relationship also arose. The attraction was too great and I proceeded to call her and ask her for a date. She initially put me off, but the next call was successful and we went out for dinner.

There was an immediate bilateral attraction and affectionate closeness that quickly progressed to a marital like intimacy.

We both became desirous of living together, but her three children would be accompanying her and our present quarters were too small. One day I told her that we would live together if she could find a rental unit suitable for all of us and remain in the area. The next day when I joined her after work, I knew then that things were becoming serious when she informed me that she had found a suitable house. We visited the house and moved in a few days later.

That was the very beginning of a relationship that has now covered forty years, all starting from a routine office visit.

THE BEST NEIGHBORHOOD YET

In the early days of Pam and my romance, we dated and were seen publicly as an attractive couple. This was many years before the sexual revolution which allowed for premarital unions and conjugal relationships without the marriage ceremony. We obeyed the social rules for the first part of our relationship and were active in the community as a couple. However, the interpersonal portion of our togetherness began to demand more.

Pam was living in a fairly populated area of Morgan City, with her three children in a small, three-bedroom house and close neighbors. I would visit frequently for dinners and romance. I was a well-known, young doctor at that time and always took care to depart at an acceptable time.

We both had been married twice before and were determined not to enter another relationship permanently without first testing it with some living together time. Pam was beginning to push for a closer union and I was agreeable, but somewhat fearful of creating a reputation damaging situation. Finally, I relented and told her, "If you can find us a house in a rather isolated neighborhood, where we won't stand out like two sore thumbs we can move in together."

Knowing East St. Mary Parish, I thought it would take several weeks to months for her to accomplish this task. Three days later, she informed me, "I have found a house and neighborhood which I think would work. It's in the west end of Patterson, in a small neighborhood which is not highly populated, and we can drive out and look at it today."

Very surprised, I replied, "I'm sure that it won't be suitable, but we can drive out and look at it after work this afternoon," which we did.

The area was indeed isolated, being on a "U" shaped street, with only one to two houses on each side. The house she found was at the entrance and was surrounded by a forest of cane, which completely shielded the house from street view. The only part meeting the street was the driveway. The next step was moving in, which Pam accomplished in two days.

The neighborhood was perfect and we lived there without attracting any attention or making neighbor acquaintances. We lived in the delightful area for almost two years until we purchased and moved into Idlewild Plantation House on December 24, 1976.

A MERRY CHRISTMAS, THE FIRST OF MANY

We had been in the market for a house for some time, but nothing met our wishes until Idlewild, a pre-Civil War home on the lower Atchafalaya River, suddenly came up for sale. Since my teenage years, I had always dreamed of living in an antebellum home. As the result of an assignment in high school, to draw a picture of the house we wanted to live in when we grew up, I had drawn a picture of an old home with columns.

I was familiar with Idlewild and its history, as I had been the family doctor of the Seyberns, the family that had lived in the house and whose ancestors first purchased the house in 1867. Pam and I contacted the realtor and did a current close-up inspection. The old home needed some work, but we both loved it, so an offer was made somewhat less than the asking price. After several back and forth offers, a final price was offered which was above our top comfortable price. Sadly, I informed Pam that we would not be living in our dream house.

Christmas was approaching and we were still living in the small rental house in Patterson. The thought of what a wonderful Christmas present to all the house would be, prompted me to make another slightly higher offer. Much to my surprise, it was quickly accepted three days before Christmas. I chose to keep this a secret and didn't tell Pam.

On Christmas Eve, as we drove near the house, after buying presents and decorations, I said, "Let's walk around the yard and look at Idlewild one last time."

With tears in her eyes, Pam replied, "I'm not sure that's a good idea," as I turned into the driveway.

We walked around the yard under the huge live oaks and then along the riverfront. As we returned to the front, I asked, "Why don't we look inside once more?"

We climbed up the steps and peered through the windows near the front door.

"Let's look inside so we won't forget it," I said.

"Do you have a key?" she replied.

"Try the door, it's probably not locked."

She pulled on the screen door and it opened. Then I turned the knob and opened the wooden door. I then lifted her in my arms and carried her over the threshold, into the living room.

"Merry Christmas and I hope we spend many more here," I said.

"What are you doing? What are you talking about?" she asked.

I explained the results of my last offer and watched the excitement build.

"We must get our Christmas tree and the kids and come back here to celebrate Christmas Eve," she cried.

We rushed to the rent house, explained the happiness to the young ones, gathered the presents and the undecorated tree and returned to Idlewild.

The old house was empty of furniture and fortunately had old space heaters and electricity in each room. We gathered in the west downstairs bedroom, closed the doors and lit the heater. We placed the tree in front of the old fireplace and decorated it. We opened presents, sang Christmas carols, enjoyed family closeness and spent the first Christmas in our new old home.

Everyone was happy except Pam's youngest child, Felisa, a five-year-old. With a plaintive voice, she asked, "How will Santa know where to deliver my tricycle? He won't know the Christmas tree is in this old house."

We reassured her. After Felisa was asleep, we returned to the rent house and we assembled her tricycle and took it back to Idlewild and placed it next to the Christmas tree.

We were awakened Christmas morning by Felisa crying, "My tricycle isn't here. Let's go to the old house and see if Santa delivered it there."

Happiness returned when she saw the decorated tree with her new tricycle next to it.

MARRIAGE OF A LIFETIME

Pam and I had been living together, unmarried, for two years, back in the seventies before that was more acceptable as the fashionable thing to do. We had both been married twice before and had agreed to do a test run before sealing our union legally. Things were going very well as the day was approaching when we had first met. We had a spontaneous agreement to wed on August 21, 1977, two years from that first meeting day.

We had been living in the antebellum home, Idlewild, on the banks of the lower Atchafalaya in the little town of Patterson, when shortly after the date decision, Pam approached me with a request, "Do you think we could have the wedding and celebration at Idlewild?"

"If you plan, prepare and do everything needed and notify me when it's complete, I'll show up," I replied.

That's all it took to get the ball rolling and Pam began researching weddings held during the antebellum period. Money was a scarcity at that time, and Pam overseeing and performing most of the duties saved a great deal. She almost lived on her sewing machine, making the bridesmaids' dresses for our daughters, Susan and Felisa. Her bridal dress was made by a dressmaker in New Orleans, under her direction to resemble that of Scarlett O'Hara of "Gone with the Wind" fame.

The wedding cake was to be an outstanding accomplishment that Pam made after learning from old cookbooks. It had five layers made in iron skillets, from large to small size, with each layer being of different type; vanilla, chocolate, lemon, coconut and spice. Different homemade jellies were placed between the layers to hold them in place and to further enhance the delicious flavors. Decorative roses, made of meringue, were placed around the cake to make it stand out even more. Upon completion, the cake was huge, but would feed the crowd we expected.

As usual, the unexpected always happen. The day of the wedding, with the cake sitting majestically in the middle of the dining room table, it began to lean. Immediately Pam held the cake and instructed me, "Walt, go to the hardware store and get some wooden dowels that we can push through the cake from the top down to support it. Hurry!"

"All right," I replied. "Can you hold it until I get back?"

"No problem," she replied.

I hurried to Cardinals Hardware Store, gathered the wooden dowels and rushed back home to find Pam still supporting the cake with her hands.

"Wash those dowels and hurry back here, and I'll direct you in what to do," she said.

As I approached the table with the dowels in hand, Pam instructed me, "I'm going to straighten the cake, and then you push them through from the top."

I performed my task, but when Pam removed her hands, the cake returned to a leaning position, though much less. She was most distressed as she always desires perfection. I entered some humor and informed her, "Don't worry, it still looks great and we'll have a name for our famous cake, "The Leaning Tower of Patterson.

My main task was to design and send the invitations, and many were sent as we had become somewhat prominent in the Tri-City community and had many friends. The invitation was unique and read,

At 5:00 p.m. on August 21, 1977, At Idlewild
We will legitimize our union
We would be happy and honored
If you would join us this
Festive occasion for the ceremony
And the reception to follow

The attendance was overwhelming, and we gathered in the yard under a huge oak tree, that henceforth became known as "The Marrying Tree."

I accompanied Judge Buddy Fleming and we awaited the bridesmaids, who had just walked from the house facing the river. As we waited in the shade of the Marrying Tree, Pam walked majestically toward me, accompanied by her two sons, who presented her to me. Judge Fleming performed a memorable ceremony and then everyone entered the house, eating the cake and other delicacies. The upper floor had been decorated and a small band, composed of schoolmates of our sons, played music for the festive reception. Drinking, dancing and eating continued until late into the night when we had our first married night together.

The next day, we left for a wonderful honeymoon, following the Natchez Trace, camping out and sometimes, sleeping in our van. We returned early, out of necessity, to greet an approaching hurricane.

It has truly been the "Marriage of a Lifetime."

A PICTURE FOREVER PRECIOUS

I have taken thousands of photographs in my lifetime. Beginning in my youthful days when I would use my mother's old metal Kodak camera. Those pictures have covered accomplishments, loved ones, friendships, adventures and a multiplicity of things, as well as many taken by others at my direction. To pick one out and assign it the importance of being the photo that I would select as being the one that would be saved above all others takes a bit of thought and remembrance. After a great deal of research, I came upon that photograph.

The selection of me placing the wedding ring on my bride's finger stood out as one of the tops for a number of reasons. The picture symbolized the finality and commitment we were both making to the remainder of our life together. As this was the third time for each of us, this was a most important event. We had worked at making this last the remainder of our life. We had cohabited for over a year and this was at a time when it was not socially acceptable to live together out of wedlock. We also both had children from previous marriages that came with the union.

The success of putting all of this together confirmed to us that we were meant for each other.

The background of the photo also reflects the importance that we had assigned to this event. Good friends and their children, as well as relatives, joined us under the oak trees in the yard of our antebellum plantation home, Idlewild. We had chosen this site because we both wanted to live in this wonderful home and grounds for the rest of our life.

The main focus of the picture reflects the marriage document being read by Judge Buddy Fleming. The seriousness of my saying the vows and placing the ring, as well as the onlooker's expressions also makes this obvious. But, the expression on Pam's face tells more than anything else. She was so touched by my vows and the situation that she limited her response to a simple, "I do", for fear of crying.

After all of the mental and physical searching, it is obvious that this picture is surely more than just a photograph. It is totally due to the meaning it reflects. The one fact that gives it such a place in the selection process, is that thirty-nine years later, all the reasons for the photo being taken still persist.

THE BEST NAME

After all of the weird names of weird things, this one has to be tops.

Years ago when my Texas wife, Pam, and I were first married, and she only knew how to peel and eat crawfish, she saw my brother Carly running his mud boat in the flooded rice field near the small Cajun town of Gueydan.

Entranced by this strange endeavor, she asked, "Do you think Carly would take me crawfishing?"

When asked, my brother said, "Certainly, but you must learn how to do it. This isn't a tour, it's a job and I need to make money. There will be three of us in the boat, all with a job and title. I will sit in the back steering the boat and I am the "Captain". Walter will sit up front and when I steer the boat up to the trap, he will lift it, empty the crawfish into the container and he is the "Trap Man". You will be in the center, receiving the empty trap. Your job will be to place bait in the trap and replace it in the water. Your title will be the "Master Baiter".

Needless to say Pam never went crawfishing. However, we have spent many enjoyable moments fishing, duck hunting and boating together in and around coastal Morgan City.

ONCE IN A LIFETIME

My wife, Pam, and I have been very fortunate in our life together to have traveled the world over. We have taken trips to many countries, which were so enjoyable, that Pam developed her motto to me, "I will be ready to go anywhere in the world with you, if you give me twenty-four hours notice".

As our twentieth anniversary approached, I decided to do something special and garner a stock of "Good Husband Points". We were spending a weekend in New Orleans and I had made us a reservation at a nice non-tourist restaurant on Magazine Street, where we had never eaten before. Pam was very excited and impressed that I had done this as a surprise and my "Points" began.

We were seated and I had ordered champagne without Pam noticing this. The waiter served us, filling our glasses, after which I lifted my glass in a toast and said, "Here is to our twentieth anniversary and many more to follow and as a special celebration, you have twenty-four hours to prepare for us to fly to New York." As she laughed excitedly, I continued, "We will spend one night there and the next morning, we will depart for Paris for a two week stay. Our flight to Paris will be extra special aboard the Concorde."

Pam was so excited and thrilled that she shed tears of happiness and needless to say, my "Good Husband Points" were so numerous, they would never be used up, and I still use them today.

At that time the Concorde, owned by France and Britain, was the most famous and luxurious airplane in the world. It was spectacular because of its supersonic speed and 'Avant-garde' looks. In a normal passenger jet, the trip from New York to Paris was eight hours. In the Concorde, it was three and one half.

The next two days were non-stop in preparation. I had extended Pam's motto by twenty-four hours because of the duration and extent of the trip. She was not late and we flew from New Orleans to New York on time. We took in a Broadway Play that night and awakened the next morning with great excitement. A short cab drive took us to the Air France section of J.F.K. Airport, where we checked in at the counter.

There began the special treatment we were to receive until we reached Paris. As soon as we presented our tickets and the attendant noted we were to be passengers on the Concorde, she said a few words into the phone in French and very shortly we were informed that we would be escorted to the private lounge. Then a young man in uniform attentively escorted us down a private hallway into a very lush private lounge with all the accoutrements one would expect in a special French restaurant. Waitresses in stylish uniforms served us champagne and directed us to a buffet with many different choices.

Looking through the windows of the lounge, we were seeing the real Concorde for the first time. We had seen pictures of this airplane in the past, but to see the real thing up close was stunning. The nose, wings and all parts of this supersonic jet were obviously made for speed. The cockpit sat above everything else in the nose of the plane, which moved after take-off, to allow more speed.

We then began to board, walking down a closed-in private passageway. Unexpectedly, the passenger cabin inside was rather small. It held ninety-two passengers and six pilots and attendants. All seats were first class, with two on each side of the center aisle.

We were given the usual instructions, which included informing us about a strange meter on the wall separating the passenger section and cockpit. It was rectangular, about two feet wide and one-foot high, with a zero lit up inside. This was the Mach Meter. It measured the jet's speed in relation to the speed of sound, with Mach 1 being that speed approximately five hundred miles per hour.

The Concorde then began to taxi out on the runway as we prepared to depart. Our seats had a round window on the wall next to us, allowing us to view the area as we rapidly became airborne. Immediately off the ground, the Concorde began to ascend rapidly at a very steep angle and we were shoved back against our seats by the centrifugal force. We could feel the loose skin on our cheeks being forced back on the bones, as though a hurricane force wind was being encountered. The Mach Meter registered 1 and continued to rise. As it approached Mach 2, our ascent became less steep and smoother and we leveled off at 60,000 feet, nearly twelve miles' altitude. At this height, we were privileged to view a sight very few people get to see in their lifetime. Looking out the window, we saw a clear sky with a curved horizon, which took us a moment to understand. We were looking at the Earth's curvature. What a sight!

Now the plane was flying smoothly and the attendants were up and serving everyone champagne and hors d'oeuvres. They also gave us a certificate signed by the Captain, our attendant and the Chairman of the Concorde Board, certifying that we had broken the sound barrier on board the Concorde. Accompanying this were two menus, one for food and one for wine. The food, of course, began with caviar. The wine menu stated that these were selected by wine specialists each month for the Concorde clientele and it began with a Cuvee Special Champagne and went through four other ten-year old wines.

The services and consumption of the food and drink followed by a short nap, and we found ourselves beginning the descent into Charles de Gaulle Airport in Paris. The descent was uneventful, but because of our height, it lasted nearly an hour. The landing was smooth and swift and we were shortly exiting into another luxurious private lounge, to which our luggage was delivered.

We spent the next two weeks living in a walk-up flat in a Parisian neighborhood. We lived like the natives, having wine in the outdoor restaurants lining the Champs Elyseés and shopping for food and French bread at the open street market, less than two blocks from our apartment. Near the last day of our sojourn, Pam wanted to do some fashionable shopping, so we spent our day in an exclusive shopping area. While strolling around, we were approached by an English speaking gentleman, who had obviously heard us conversing in English. He asked us, "Did you hear the terrible news about Princess Diana?" He informed us of her death and the circumstances surrounding it. He also told us that she was staying at the hotel in the middle of our shopping area and had left it only a short time before the accident.

We returned home on the Concorde.

On July 25, 2000, as the Concorde was taking off, it struck an object on the runway, caught on fire and crashed, killing all 109 people on the plane and four on the ground. This was publicly unneeded, as the Concorde had been unprofitable since its inception and it became even more so.

On November 26, 2003, the Concorde was retired to an air museum, never to fly again.

AROUND THE WORLD IN TEN YEARS

Since Pam and I first met, one of the things that has kept us close and attracted to each other is our adventurous spirit. This has led us into travels around the world starting in the late 70's. The most extensive ten-year period was started with our trip on the Concorde to Paris in 1997. All of our trips have been adventures, but traveling to one of the most unique cities in the world, on board the most unique airplanes in the world and spending two weeks in a Parisian neighborhood makes that trip one of the tops.

One of our longest trips was to China where we traveled up the Yangtze River to the newly built, largest dam in the world. Visiting the most populated country in the world and getting to view the Great Wall, one of the World's Wonders, and the Terra Cotta soldiers, as well as mingling with people who were very eager to speak to us "round eyes" in our own language, gave our China visit a uniqueness unexcelled.

A spin-off trip to Thailand, after China, enabled us to see a country of humble people who were very religious. Their native dancing and ornate costumes entertained us.

Visit to the historic country of Italy was enlightening, especially to see things we had studied and heard about all of our life. The Leaning Tower of Pisa, all of the ancient Roman architecture and history, as well as a trip to the Vatican and being blessed by the Pope, along with the throngs gathered in St. Peter's Square, make it all unforgettable.

Rotary International has enhanced our travelogue as we have been to several of the International Conventions held in a different country every four years.

Our trip to Brazil enabled us to see another Wonder of the World, the Iguazu Falls, a group of seven waterfalls extending across the country border into Argentina, and another country visited. The flight was not as long as to China, but nearly so.

We attended another Rotary Convention in 2002 in Barcelona, Spain. Besides touring a beautiful city and making a side trip, day tour to Portugal, we were fortunate to have the experience of a lifetime when we were selected to oversee the backstage accommodations of the former President of Russia, Mikhail Gorbachev, who was a featured speaker at the convention. We even had our pictures taken with him.

During that ten-year period, we reached the peak of our snow skiing experiences and traveled to the Alps and skied in Zermatt, Switzerland and Northern Italy.

Those ten years passed with an unwelcome speed. Like the Concorde, we too have retired.

BUONO FORTUNA IN ROME

Our trip to Italy was one of a lifetime. Visiting the Leaning Tower, the canals of Venice, Tuscany and the Island of Sicily makes it difficult to rate one above all, until you encounter Rome. The entanglement in world history, architecture that remains outstanding and the ability to mingle with the population continues to maintain Rome as the "go to" city in the world.

In April 1993, Pam and I traveled to Rome and booked into the small fifteen room Hotel Olympic, located in the center of the city. The few rooms in the miniature hotel was matched by their size, but this was compensated for by its location within walking distance of many castles, the Colosseum and the Vatican.

The Colosseum tour was the most informative and emotional of all visits. Walking through areas that housed lions and tigers, and visiting the shafts of elevators that transported these wild creatures up to the main floor, where they were freed to feed upon human sacrifices to the delight of thousands of spectators, brought feelings of pity and sadness even though it occurred centuries ago.

Sitting and standing in areas once occupied by Roman emperors, who allowed life or death to gladiators who had lost their battle, brought a feeling of the present rather than antiquity. Despite being ancient, the Colosseum reminds one of our present day football stadiums, less the bloodshed.

The great location of our small hotel allowed us to walk to the nearby fountains and piazzas, which were gathering places. Individual and small groups of musicians and various food stuff enabled us to mingle with the locals.

We learned that Mass was held in St. Peter's Square each Sunday, so we made plans to attend this auspicious event. That morning, as we made our way toward St. Peter's, we noted greater numbers of people joining us and we heard different languages all of the way. Hearing nearby walkers speaking English, we asked, "Why are so many people on the street? Is this unusual?"

"Yes, they answered. "Today is a special saint's day and the Pope will be saying Mass."

The square was filled when we entered and our standing area was over a quarter mile away, but we could see that the steps of St. Peter's Cathedral were set up as an altar and Cardinals were gathering. The crowd was immense and the only thing outnumbering the humans were the pigeons, which flew around in large flocks with some landing on the scattered structures.

The Pope said Mass and the numerous priests scattered through the crowd administering Communion. By this time Pam became fatigued and walked a short distance to sit away from the throng. The Pope gave his sermon in seven languages and Mass was complete, and the crowd began to depart.

I walked back toward Pam, who was surrounded by a group of people, all standing and animatedly chanting, "Buono Fortuna, Buono Fortuna." (Good Fortune, Good Fortune)

As I approached Pam, she was frowning and wiping her hair with a cloth.

"What's wrong," I asked.

"I don't understand this culture. They wish you "Good Fortune, Good Fortune, when a pigeon dumps in your hair."

A FLAT IN PARIS

Do you want the experience of a lifetime? If you do, you must focus your time, money and sense of adventure. You must devote at least two weeks or longer and substantial dollars and let your free spirit fly as you plan a vacation in Paris. This is a trip where you won't be a tourist staying in a posh hotel, but a Parisian living in a small apartment in a neighborhood composed of native French Parisians.

To ensure this journey will be pleasant, it will help to speak a little French, even if it is Cajun. The ability to communicate in a native language opens many doors. One must at least not harbor the misconceptions of many Americans, that the French are haughty and self-centered. This false premise is fostered by American tourists in France who walk up to a native, and in English ask, "Where is the Eiffel Tower?"

The response being a look of lack of understanding, a "nod" and a walking away. The feeling is they are not friendly and we never think how we would respond in opposite circumstances.

A little "Pardon" or "Bon Jour" is most appropriate.

A perfect neighborhood is found by taking the Metro to Rue Monge in the St. Germain area, having made arrangements with the rental company to show you an apartment. It is important to scout the neighborhood in advance and to view the flat and surroundings for noise level and convenience.

Typical of the St. Germain is a second floor walk-up. This is cheaper than a hotel room and is composed of a coded entrance door, a two flight walk-up to a studio room with a separate toilet and a main room approximately 15 x 12 feet. It is furnished by a couch that makes into a bed, a small breakfast table and T.V. A 6 x 9' kitchen containing a sink, cabinets, refrigerator, dishwasher and stove.

Two blocks away is located a typical neighborhood market of Parisian necessities, food and wine. These markets are unique in that much of the food is prepared and only requires cooking. Featured in this market are stuffed escargot, various meat and poultry dishes, as well as fresh asparagus, artichokes marinated in olive oil and herbs, cous cous and many inexpensive excellent French wines. Daily shopping allows preparation of excellent fresh dishes with wines before, during and after dinner.

The Metro system of transportation is outstanding in the world. Underground stations are located every few blocks with maps available to enable city-wide travel. It is inexpensive and convenient, well-kept and well used. World class sightseeing can all be done by Metro.

The Eiffel Tower is one of the "must see' attractions and the open elevator ride to the top is breathtaking. The view from the apex is one that few will forget.

A trip to the Bois de Boulogne, a 2200- acre park on the outer area of Paris, is most rewarding, especially on weekends. In the spring and early summer, roses of all varieties are abundant. A nice lake attracts row boats with many females attempting to row. From ballerinas practicing under the trees to Frisbee throwing youngsters, the park is bustling. The amusement center features the world's largest Ferris wheel.

One may hear more English when touring the Royal Chateau, than in any area of the city with portable audio tours available. The Chateau was built at the directions of Louis XIV, the Sun King, and shows the elaborate richness for which he is famous. The Kings Quarters, the Queens Quarters, the Hall of Mirrors and the Apartments, as the rooms are called, are decorated with original furniture and styles of the times. The lavishness of the furnishings and living conditions of people residing in the Chateau was sumptuous by any standards.

The advantage of the neighborhood flat is that after a tiring day of touring, one can stop by the market on the way home. Veal stew, marinated cheese sprinkled broccoli, a cheese stuffed pastry roll heated and topped with an excellent Vin Rouge is so simple. Chocolate cake and Crème Brule are always available as dessert before bedtime and, of course, a good Vin Blanc.

The Champs Elyseés, the most famous roadway in Paris and the world, can take days to explore. Walking, with guide book in hand, can easily take the place of formal expensive tours. Having a glass of wine, seated at a sidewalk café is an important and fun part of the day. The Champs is an excellent area for eating out or formal dining. In Paris, dining out is part of the culture and poor restaurants are unheard of, so one can just walk down the Champs, spot a restaurant that looks nice and partake of a gourmet meal with excellent wine and service.

Couture, dress design and dress making, is high fashion in Paris. Areas of the city are designated for this industry with stores that sell the goods. If you travel in June or July, you will be able to get large discounts as this is the end of the season. Surprisingly none of the discounted apparel bears the label with the designer's name, such as Armani, Channel or St. Lauren.

A word of caution is needed to prepare the walking traveler in Paris from excess foot fatigue. One must look and take care to avoid dog feces. Parisians love their dogs and take them everywhere. The dogs, as a whole, are extremely well mannered and very unobtrusive. They are present in restaurants, on the Metro, on the streets, in the markets, in cabs, cars, handheld carrying cases zip closed and most frequently, on leashes. Dogs riding the Metro must pay a fee determined by their size. But, with all the dogs, their "poo" is evident. It is present in the street in piles. One statistician estimated that pedestrians step in dog "poo" once every two hundred forty-seven footsteps. Avoid the "Plague de Paris."

A last travel tip to make your trip easier is to travel lightly. Do not pack more than three days of clothing which can be mix matched. Clothes can be washed or taken to the cleaners on a long trip, new clothing can be purchased along with cheap luggage when returning home. This fits well with the flat in Paris.

SERVICE HAS ITS REWARDS

About twenty years ago, my wife, Pam, was an active Rotarian and approached me with her desire to go to a Rotary International Convention in Buenos Aires, Argentina. Not being a Rotarian, but loving to travel, my answer was "Great, you can go to all the meetings, but I am going to see the city and learn to Tango." Things didn't work out quite like that but I did learn to Tango. The convention showcased the things Rotary accomplished worldwide and I was so impressed that I joined Rotary when we returned to the states.

We continued going to international conventions after this and had many adventures. We flew to Tokyo, Japan and then rode the Bullet Train at two hundred sixty miles per hour to the convention site in Osaka. In San Antonio we practiced the Rotary motto, "Service Above Self," and volunteered to be Sergeant at Arms, whose function was to be available in the venue to answer questions and direct attendees to various locations. Each time we served we wore a different uniform beginning with a cowboy hat and vest in San Antonio, to a jacket and small felt hat resembling Al Capone in Chicago. In Japan we had a red peaked cap, a red smock and a sword depicting Samurai Warriors. One of the simpler costumes was in Barcelona, Spain, where we wore a small red baseball cap and red arm band, but there we had an experience of a lifetime.

Each convention usually featured a world renowned figure as a speaker. The Barcelona Convention had Jerry Lewis, the comedian and worldwide promoter of funds for treatment of Muscular Dystrophy. The other prominent figure was the former president and leader of the Soviet Union, Mikhail Gorbachev.

The Sergeant at Arm duties on speaker's day would usually encompass aiding proper seating by country and directing traffic of attendees. Because of our tenure as S.A.A. at previous conventions, we were well known to supervisor, Mike McCullough. He took me aside before the meeting and asked if Pam and I would be in charge of the Green Room. We learned that this was an area behind the stage out of sight of the audience, where speakers could relax. It contained comfortable furniture, tables with snack food and drinks and toilet facilities. We gladly agreed to take this task.

The day began uneventfully with the Green Room serving a few minor speakers. I took care of the inner room needs while Pam stood outside guarding the door from intruders. Suddenly Mike darts from behind the stage toward us and says, "Clear out the Green Room, Gorbachev is coming. His room doesn't have a toilet and he has to pee. His two bodyguards will be with him." As a physician I had experienced many harrowing, frightening and exciting experiences but nothing ever like this. Looking down the poorly lit hall, I see a door open at the end. Two large men came down the hall walking and looking into every door and nook. These men were obviously the bodyguards straight from the KGB, Russia's secret service. They were over six and one half feet tall, very muscular, wearing coats and ties and each carried a suitcase.

Pam asked somewhat fearfully, "What do you think is in their suitcases?"

I responded in the same tone, "Probably guns."

The guards then approached us, looking quite menacing and fearless. Only one of them spoke English and he asked, "Where is Mr. Gorbachev to go?" I opened the door to the Green Room and they entered like their guns were drawn. They searched the whole area and then exited going back down the hall, where they opened the door speaking Russian. Out stepped the man known to the whole world, a short, chubby and near bald fellow with a red birth mark on his scalp. Here was the gentleman, who a short time ago was one of the three most important and powerful men in the world, walking toward us. I entered the Green Room opening the door as the bodyguards came in motioning me to the area behind the door. Then Gorbachev entered going straight to the toilet. A short time later he walked back into the room, glancing at me and then partaking of the snacks.

I'm watching all of this awestruck, thinking, "Who would have ever dreamed that a boy from the little Cajun town of Gueydan, would be in the same room and overlooking the care of such a world known important person." I shivered. Then my normal thinking returned. I had a small camera in my pocket and feeling it I wondered about getting a picture. I was afraid to take one without permission, so I walked over to the English speaking guard and asked, holding my camera in hand. "Do you think Mr. Gorbachev would mind if you took a picture of me standing next to him?"

He replied, "I believe it will be all right, but let me ask him." He walked over speaking Russian and Gorbachev looked over at me with that well known dead pan expression and nodded. I walked over handing my camera as Gorbachev stood and I had the picture of a lifetime. Then they prepared to depart.

Pam had been outside guarding the door and was standing across the hall as we exited the Green Room. I thought, "I wonder if I can get a picture of Mr. Gorbachev with Pam?" Holding my camera, I walked toward Pam while looking toward Gorbachev. As he glanced toward me, I held the camera in the snapping position, while gesturing toward him and then Pam with a questioning look on my face. Again with total lack of emotion he nodded yes. Pam scampered up next to him and I took the second picture of a lifetime.

This has always been one of the most unforgettable, important and exciting experiences of my life and it all happened because of "Service Above Self."

MORGAN CITY ROTARY CLUB AND THE R.I. CONVENTION IN NEW ORLEANS

The Rotary International (R.I.) Convention was scheduled to be in New Orleans in 2007, but was cancelled due to damage from Hurricane Katrina. My wife, Pam Daniels was Past Club President and past District Governor (PDG). She and PDG Billy Foster from Houma were on the Host Organization Committee (HOC) for the cancelled convention and were reappointed to the HOC for the 2011 convention. PDG Foster was in charge of the House of Friendship (HOF) and asked Pam to be his chair in charge of designing and decorating the HOF. PDG Foster had experienced Pam's talents when he was District Governor in 1998 and he asked Pam to begin Rotary Youth Leadership Award (RYLA) Camp. She formed the camp and it has been a success every summer since.

The HOF is one of the most important venues of the convention, as it is a gathering place for Rotarian attendees from around the world. Here they can have fellowship, entertainment, food and visit numerous booths featuring Rotarian projects and functions.

Local Rotarian Jim Firmin and spouse, Yan Ming, created a booth advertising his China School Project, thereby exposing it to over 20,000 Rotarians. There were 500 booths featuring such things as the Fellowship of Physicians, the Fellowship of Sailing Rotarians, as well as numerous ones featuring Rotary Service Projects.

Pam's job began early, as the HOC began meeting in New Orleans two years before the convention. Quarterly meetings became monthly, and then weekly, as opening day approached. Chair people of all functions, from volunteers to finance, to sales, met and gave reports and discussed possible improvements. I was the present Club President and accompanied my wife, Pam, and helped out as convention neared.

As PDG, Pam also traveled to many clubs in the District, urging attendance and volunteering for help at the convention. This was very successful and stirred up enthusiasm in our own club, which had donated $20 per member to help defray convention costs. Our club members were stimulated to attend the convention and be a part of it.

As the convention loomed, Pam's work increased. She drew up a blueprint of the HOF, which was used by the architects to lay out the HOF in the New Orleans Morial Convention Center. She also engaged entertainment and scheduled performances in the four stages of the HOF. One of the featured performers was Scott Burke, our grandson and RYLA graduate, and his friend, who stilt walked eight feet high and juggled in Uncle Sam and Court Jester costumes. They traversed the HOF and were crowd favorites.

The HOF covered 209,000 square feet and opening day was started with a Mardi Gras Parade, which Pam designed and produced. The parade was led by a high stepping drum major and the Pin Stripe Brass Band, followed by two small floats carrying the dignitaries. Following that was a bevy of our club volunteers, who paraded around the entire 90,000 square foot HOF.

Leading off were Grand Maids, Mimi Brooks and Donna Meyers, dressed in their costumes from past Krewe of Galatea parades, as they followed the first float. Behind the second float were Natalie and Mike Hayes from West Lake Club, costumed as a Duke and Duchess. Following them were PDG Lance Linscomb and his daughter, King and Queen from Lafayette. Our club members, Rose and Steve Arceneaux, followed resplendent in their King and Queen costumes, from Berwick. The main portion of the parade was followed by second liners, led by Carla Prejean strutting her stuff, waving her white handkerchief.

The parade was a huge success with participants handing out beads and toys to Rotarians, who had never seen a Mardi Gras Parade, but quickly learned, "Throw me something, mister." Filming all of this in motion picture was our faithful club photographer, Stephen Breaux.

As a moneymaker to help finance the HOF was a store called "The Cajun Cottage." The small building was in the motif of an old Cajun house with a rickety wooden fence surrounding it. Various goods, ranging from New Orleans memorabilia to Rotary wear, was available. Our banking club members, Diana Irvin and Joanne Bergeron, donned different hats and became volunteer sales ladies, thoroughly enjoying their tasks.

Part of every R.I. Convention is an event called "Host Hospitality Night" (HHN), where local Rotarians invite visiting Rotarians to their homes, or out to dinner, or to a special function. Members of our club joined with the Houma, Thibodeaux, Golden Meadow and Grand Isle clubs to put on "A Night in Cajun Land' at South Down Plantation in Houma. The Rotarian guests from the world over were picked up at their hotels in New Orleans and transported by police escorted buses the approximately 50 miles. Upon arrival, they were greeted and joined a second line as they departed their bus, and were danced to the plantation house and grounds. There they were met by all of the participating clubs, cooking and serving their most famous dish. Our club prepared and served white beans and fried catfish.

Dean Duplantis and his wife Susan, Mike Bezard, Luke Manfre, Rob Radtke and Ricky Romaire were the volunteers, cooks and servers, who transported all the fish filets, thirty pounds of prepared white beans and all the cooking paraphernalia. Rob brought his cooking trailer, which had all the necessary tools and appliances for cooking on the spot. The trip was over tiring, and upon arrival there was not a great deal of enthusiasm, until Ricky opened his ice chest in the back of the truck. A few beers later, they were all festive. Dean, Susan and Mike did most of the serving while Ricky, Rob and Luke kept the fish available. Their fried catfish and white beans were a crowd pleaser with frequent second servings.

A possible problem was brought to fore when a lady from India asked, "What is a catfish?" Dean explained that it was a common fish in Louisiana that had big whiskers. With a little fear of missed appeal in the translation, the "cat" was dropped and we were serving "fried fish."

A small Cajun band, with a fiddler and singer, were entertaining. Some people danced and everyone ate. The function was extremely successful and many slept on their bus back to New Orleans. All participants agreed that this event was a highlight of their trip.

Two weeks after the convention concluded, a meeting of the HOC including R. I. President Klingsmith and his R. I. Convention Chairman, Ron Burton, was held in New Orleans to critique the convention and present awards. It was a well-attended cocktail party in a French Quarter restaurant. Pam was awarded a large crystal engraved plaque for designing. "The Best House of Friendship Ever as Chair of the Decorating Committee, New Orleans, 2011."

At our club assembly, held to assess the convention, all members who attended or participated in the convention presented their thoughts, feelings and descriptions of their experience. Upon completion, those members who had not attended, wished they had.

Our club contributed more, had more attendees and participated more than any other club in our district.

IDLEWILD PLANTATION

***

THE FIRST AND LAST HOUSE

I was brought into this world in our family home in the Pure Oil Camp by Dr. G. L. Gardiner, who traveled the five miles from Gueydan to perform a home delivery. Our house was one of six in the compound of the Pure Oil Company in Gueydan. The superintendent and various supervisors lived in the houses, the size of which was determined by their position in the hierarchy. Our home was one of the smaller ones, but still comfortable.

The house had a living room, dining room, kitchen, two bedrooms and a bathroom. My brother, Carly, and I inhabited the front bedroom, which abutted the front porch which had a swing. My mother and father resided in the back bedroom, which contained the only fan in the house, a small oscillating fan sitting on a table adjacent to the bed, directing a flow of air to cool them.

The summer nights were horrendously hot in South Louisiana, and to this day I remember the night when a large window fan was installed and operated. The fan sucked air through open windows in the house, cooling the area. A window in the front bedroom where my brother and I slept opened just next to our bed, and the air was propelled rapidly and cooled so efficiently that we thought we might have to use a blanket.

The living room was used by the entire family with my father reading the paper or listening to the news on the radio, my mother sewing, and Carly and I ranging between our bedroom, which opened into the living room.

The dining room was rarely used except for special meals, although it had a dining table and chairs.

The kitchen was a small room containing a cook stove, refrigerator, sink and table to seat four. We ate all meals together in the kitchen while Mother cooked and served the food.

The experience of living in this house was united with the neighbors living in the other camp houses. It is also bound to the children around my age, as well as riding to school on the bus driven by Mr. Dominic Broussard. I enjoyed this treasure until age twelve, when we moved out of the camp into Gueydan.

I now reside in the other house that also influenced my life. It is an old antebellum house named Idlewild, built in 1850. My wife, Pam, and I purchased the home on December 24, 1976 and have lived here since. It has been the childhood home for some of our children and is the gathering place for all children, grandchildren, great-grandchildren, family members and friends every year when we have our yearly reunion on Thanksgiving.

The historic nature of Idlewild, as well as the stand out antebellum architecture, has fulfilled a lifetime dream. These features, and my desire to ensure the longevity of the house, prompted me to apply and have the house entered on the National Register of Historic Places, which places Idlewild in a very prestigious and historic site.

There is a deep comfort and pleasure associated with daily living here. The back porch, which was initially open and was later screened and then after Pam's persistent urging, finally glassed in, is where we spend most of our time. This area overlooks the Lower

Atchafalaya River and gives us an unencumbered view of the river and the wildlife associated with it. Cormorants and seagulls are always present and associate with brown pelicans in the fishing season.

The most prominent birds are a pair of Bald Eagles that nest and live in the forest across the river. We frequently see them flying over the river and around our house, where one lit in a large oak tree at the rear of our house.

We frequently view squirrels in the trees, as well as a mother raccoon and three of her offspring on the ground, mingling with the turtles that lay eggs along the riverside.

The most famous visitor was a Black Bear that walked through our backyard and created such an uproar, that most of Patterson stood in our side yard, watching the bear in a tree which it had climbed while fleeing from the police. This bear was so famous, as to prompt the formation of the Bear Festival in Franklin.

We also share Idlewild with friendly unexplainable experiences. When we first moved in, Pam would hear babies crying. Years later, in another episode, pictures came crashing down off the wall in the middle of the night.

The first house was where I was born and lived my early days. Idlewild is the house where I am spending my final days, and is where I will remain.

A STARTLING DISCOVERY, WITH HISTORY

Since moving into Idlewild Plantation House, an antebellum home, we have discovered several interesting antiques, none of which prepared me for the day when I discovered the most famous.

The house has been inhabited since it was built in 1850, and survived the Civil War unharmed. It was purchased by the Union Gunboat Captain, I. E. Seybern, after the war and his family of soldiers and sailors lived in it until 1976.

Idlewild is described as a raised Louisiana cottage and rests on a brick wall, elevating it five feet off the ground, forming a space similar to a cellar. This area was used to house slaves and for the century and a half following the war, it was a storage facility. This made it a treasure trove for my inquisitive searching.

Shortly after we moved into the house, I was under it cleaning out junk and trash that had accumulated since its birth. In a remote corner was a stack of wooden planks that I began to carry outside. As I approached the bottom, I spotted what appeared to be a piece of metal. The possibilities of what it might be flashed through my mind, creating an emotional uproar. My trembling hand grasped the object and withdrew a sword. I immediately knew this to be historical, but I was somewhat disappointed, as the blade was only twenty inches long and appeared to have been broken, then reshaped and sharpened. The handle was very ornate and I surmised it was some type of ceremonial sword belonging to one of the inhabitants after the war.

The sword was placed in a safe area where it was stored, but identifying it was a project of many years. I took it to a sword smith and sword collectors in the French Quarter, but they could not give any clarity to the cloudy puzzle. It was not until 2009, when the house was being filmed for HGTV series, "If Walls Could Talk," that the mystery was solved. A member of the filming crew was an expert on antiquities, and her job was to identify pieces and assign a value to them. I presented the sword to her and informed her that we didn't know what type of sword it represented. Immediately, she said, "I know what that is. I evaluated one just like it a few months ago. That is a sword of the Knights of Pythias."

From her, and through further research, I discovered that the Knights of Pythias was a fraternal organization formed in 1864 to promote, "Friendship, Charity and Benevolence." With the encouragement of President Abraham Lincoln, the order of the Knights of Pythias was the first American Order ever chartered by an Act of Congress of the United States. The primary objectives, spoken by President Lincoln, were to "Uphold the government, honor the flag, reunite our brethren of the North and South, teach people to love one another and portray the sanctity of home and loved ones." Today there remain more than two thousand active lodges in the United States and Canada.

I also learned that the sword was presented to new members as they were inducted into the order. There were two types of swords, one with a long blade and was used for marching drills and parades, and one with a short blade used for display. This relieved my longstanding disappointed belief that the sword was broken and repaired.

The sword hangs prominently on a wall in our house on a special display hanger. When I give my twenty-five cent tour of the house, one of the features is the story of the Sword of the Order of the Knights of Pythias. It remains the best discovery to this date, as it reflects the attempts at healing after the Civil War.

UNEXPLAINED HAPPENINGS

After living almost four decades in a one hundred-sixty-six-year old house, we have experienced some events and occurrences that have no reasonable explanation. In our early years when we first moved into the house in 1976, Pam would occasionally hear a baby crying in other parts of the house, but never a baby was found. I always made light of these.

At that time, the boys slept and spent most of their home time upstairs. Our son, John, fifteen at the time, spent his nights on a small daybed in the middle bedroom. Shortly after moving in, he began to complain about his brother, Matt, sitting on the side of his bed, awakening him in the middle of the night. But, Matt was never there. It became so bothersome to John that he moved downstairs and his problems ceased.

I always laughed at those telling me their tales, as I never believed in ghosts or other-world happenings. Until it happened to me! All of the family was gathered around the dining room table waiting for Pam to serve supper. The center room upstairs sits above the dining room, with east and west bedrooms adjoining. The usual chatter was going on as Pam served supper, the blessing was said and we began eating. When suddenly loud footsteps began in the east upstairs bedroom, proceeded across the middle room to the downstairs entrance. We all looked at each other as the footsteps paused and then returned to the east bedroom where the footsteps began. The steps were heavy and sounded as though from someone wearing work boots.

Puzzled and somewhat irritated, I asked, "Whomever has the friend upstairs, go up and ask him to join us. This was not very thoughtful."

There was silence, until John said, "But, there is no one upstairs, Dad."

"Didn't everyone hear someone walking?" I incredulously asked. There was no dissent as I arose and said, "I will find out who did the walking."

I made my way up the stairwell and flipped the light on as I entered the center room and made my way through each room. Much to my exasperation, there was no one to be found. I even searched the adjacent attic and there was still a void.

Things remained quiet and calm, until recently. In the dark, wee morning hours, I was awakened by a loud crashing sound in the River Room, next to my bedroom. Pam was sleeping in the other bedroom with the puppies, so I had no other input as to the cause of the crash. "One of the cats must have knocked something over onto the floor," I thought. "I'll see about it when I get out of bed at daylight," as I fell back asleep.

Six a.m. rolled around and I arose, slipped on my house shoes and went into the next room. The rear wall of this room had many hanging pictures and a few shadow boxes. On the floor, in the back corner, I spotted two of these boxes next to the wall where they had been hanging.

I thought, "No way the cats could have caused that."

The larger box, one-foot square, contained two standing doves inside the glassed-in case. I looked up the wall, searching for the hook from which the box had been hanging. What I found was a surprisingly straightened hook against the wall. The back of the shadow box, with the metal piece to which the hook was attached, had been torn away.

I then bent over and picked up the smaller shadow box, which contained four eggs, one of which now lay loose and unbroken. Its wall hook was out of the wall laying on the floor and the attachment was barely hanging from the box.

These findings were most puzzling and somewhat disturbing, as the only way these boxes could have landed on the floor, with the hooks and attachments torn loose the way they were, would be the result of someone tearing them off the wall and then dropping them on the floor, producing the crash that awakened me. But, there was no one around who could have done this.

This continued to bother me, but had the makings of a good ghost story that I told to my daughter, Cissy, and her daughter, Anne, when they visited a few weeks later. They were a little apprehensive, but had no problem sleeping in the bedroom on the opposite side of the house. This bedroom was under the west side upstairs bedroom, where our granddaughter, Chay, usually slept. She was away, visiting a friend at this time.

At 3:00 a.m., Pam and I were awakened by "Daddy, Daddy! Wake up! Wake up!" I opened my eyes to see Cissy and Anne leaning over me in the bed. "Daddy, you must get up. There is music playing upstairs," Cissy said.

Somewhat befuddled, I asked, "What are you talking about?

"Daddy, we were awakened just a short time ago by loud, unusual music coming from the bedroom above us, and it's still playing. Get up and let's go up there and find out what is going on."

I arose and led everyone to the bottom of the stairwell, where we could hear loud, booming-type music. As we went up the stairs and approached the bedroom, the music became louder. The emptiness of the upstairs made the music louder and frightening, as the booming continued.

As we entered the bedroom, I flipped on the light and immediately noted granddaughter Chay's boom box, playing in the center of the room, the area where she would sit and listen to music when she was home. The sound was from the radio, as no cd was present. I turned off the boom box without touching anything else, and we all went to bed.

The next day when Chay returned home and heard the story, she returned downstairs after checking things out.

"Are you all certain this was boom-type music?" she asked. "Because the radio is tuned to a country/western station."

Another unexplained happening.

HE JUST LAY IN THE YARD

Over the years I have become a cat lover and have acquired many, giving them names from Bobtail, Puddin, Sudio, Mignon, Pitiful Pearl, Whiska and Chat Blanc. The names usually described something distinctive about each feline, like Pitiful Pearl, who was named Pearl when she was a newborn but developed the descriptive adjective as she became older and uglier.

More than twenty years ago, I received a gift that will be with me forever. My daughter, Felisa had a beautiful white kitten that she cared for like a mother. One day she said to me, knowing I loved cats, "Daddy, my job is moving me to Houston for three months, would you care for my kitten?"

"O.K." I replied, with little thought.

Three months was not lengthy, as I fell in love with the cat, who became mine and I became his. The bond between us was immediate and he trained me well. His color was a solid, deep white and in searching for a name I came up with "Chat Blanc" or White Cat in English. It was a perfect name and fit him for his twenty-two-year lifetime.

As the kitten matured, he let me know that he didn't want to be house confined. I soon learned that his plaintive cries near the back door signaled the need for my presence. Approaching, I would find Chat Blanc standing on his hind legs with his forepaws attempting to turn the door knob to open the door. My completing the task was always greeted by a distinct meow, as he pounced out into the backyard. He also taught me to let him back in when he peered into the glassed rear door.

My lap became "cat heaven" as Chat Blanc, after eating, would climb up with a loud purr and go to sleep. If I moved before he awakened, that was greeted by snarls, showing his displeasure while he dug his claws into my clothing, attempting to remain on my lap.

Over the years, we had another cat that was dropped off at our driveway. A large long-haired black cat with a white face and paws and long distinctive white whiskers, hence his name, Whiska. My wife, Pam came upon Whiska one day when she heard this sad meow as she walked out onto the driveway. She looked up into the tree and there was a small black and white cat holding onto a limb. As she held her hands up in an attempt to catch him, Whiska jumped into her arms. From Hell to Heaven in one leap.

Whiska has grown to be a large cat and climbs the oak trees in our yard attempting to catch squirrels, unsuccessfully. However, he is our rat catcher and we frequently find mauled rodents near the back steps where he apparently leaves them for us.

Whiska and Chat Blanc were both neutered and were friendly to each other but never to the point of grooming each other or eating out of the same bowl and they never fought. They respected each other's territory. Whiska also participated in cat heaven, sitting on my lap. However, he obviously knew and accepted the fact that he was second in line for everything.

Chat Blanc always spent the night in the house, frequently at the foot of our bed. If something happened and he was locked outside, and with my deafness, Pam would be awakened in the wee morning hours by Chat Blanc, crying at the front porch window that was next to the head of our bed. He somehow learned to navigate outside the house, ending up in an area on the outside that was nearest to our sleeping site. There he would cry until Pam opened the living room door onto the porch, where she would be greeted by the cat, running across the porch into the house and ending up in our bedroom, on my feet. That taught us to always be certain he was in the house when we went to bed at night.

Many years passed with Chat Blanc staying healthy and reaching his twenty-second birthday. As we became older, I spent more time sitting in my easy chair, Chat Blanc spent more time on my lap, but now he developed a cuddlier maneuver. He would climb upon my lap as I was sitting, then push against my chin until I raised my head, making room for him to lay his head on my shoulder and drape his body across my chest. All of this, of course, was accompanied by loud purring.

At twenty-two years, which converted to over one hundred human years, I knew his remaining time was very limited. I immediately recognized his impending demise, when one day he just lay in the backyard. He would not get up, eat or drink or respond to my petting. His friend, Whiska, must have recognized that Chat Blanc was terminal when he made a presentation of a beheaded mouse. He placed the mouse between Chat Blanc's front paws but the offer was declined and he just lay in the yard. I awakened the next day to find my twenty-two-year-old cat companion dead. Sadly, with tears, I performed a burial into my pet graveyard and placed a headstone on his grave that read, "After twenty-two years, he just lay in the yard."

A BEAR VISITS IDLEWILD AGAIN!

My wife, Pam, and I live at the east end of Patterson, Louisiana in a 150-year-old plantation home named Idlewild. Over ten years ago we were visited by a young Black Bear who attracted a large crowd of our neighbors to our yard, when the word spread that a bear was stranded on a branch of one of our large oak trees along the riverside. I named him "A-Bear" as a humorous way to use a common last name of our Acadian country with the same pronunciation, 'Hebert'. A-Bear became so famous that he contributed to the city of Franklin, founding The Bayou Teche Bear Festival which has attracted crowds yearly since 2004.

Even though the subdivisions from Patterson, south of Hwy 90, have been plagued by Black Bears feeding off garbage cans, we never worried about another A-Bear until Friday, December 20, when our daughter, Felisa, called us from her cottage about 75 feet west of our house. With a panicky sound to her voice, she said, "Daddy, there is a bear invading the garbage can just outside my window."

Pam and I looked over the kitchen window just in time to see "A-Bear II" ramble around the rear of our carport toward the large oak tree that the first A-Bear had inhabited ten years ago.

A quick call to the Patterson Police brought them out of their patrol car, flashing lights around the yard and in the trees, only catching a glimpse of A-Bear II. They returned several times before I arose at daybreak, after a very restless night.

I carefully walked around the inside of the house, scouting the adjacent yard through the windows and found no evidence of A-Bear II. I then went out the back door, looking up into the tree where A-Bear had resided ten years ago. I immediately spotted A-Bear II reclining on the same large branch in the same tree. This was a very large bear, moving his head following us as we walked in the yard around the tree. A Patterson Police car entered the driveway and officer James Carinhas greeted us, informing us that they were assigned "Bear Supervision Duty."

They had already contracted Maria Davidson, Senior Biologist of the Louisiana Wildlife and Fisheries. She had been on the team that captured A-Bear with tranquilizer darts ten years earlier. Officer Carinhas called Maria so I could talk to her. She informed me that the procedure for dealing with tree bound errant bears had changed from ten years previous. Today, unless the bear was deemed dangerous, it was allowed to remain undisturbed, and she informed me that the bear would exit the tree after a day or two and return to its previous habitat. She advised me that they would follow that protocol if it was agreeable with me. With a little hesitance, I agreed, but somewhat concerned with a 300-pound bear in a tree in my yard. The police reassured me that they would make frequent patrols and ensure our safety.

The first twenty-four hours found us watching the bear from our kitchen windows as he moved to different positions on the large branch. The first morning the bear was still resting in the tree but the garbage can had been emptied on the ground where A-Bear II had taken in nourishment.

The remainder of the day was uneventful, with A-Bear II changing positions but remaining on his large branch. We wished him good night after moving the garbage can to the area where it would be picked up by the garbage truck.

After a more restful night's sleep, I was up at dawn and A-Bear II was gone.

We have enjoyed our A-Bear visits, but they are not welcome again.

STRANGE GUESTS ON THE BAYOU

Beneath a tree, shading the walkway from my back porch and the river wharf, is an area with a paucity of grass due to the lack of sunshine. It is neatly kept with smooth, fine dirt. There was a marked difference in the appearance that I noted one morning, as I walked out to the waterfront for my morning meditation. It was unusual and I had never seen the number of excavations into the dirt, leaving small mounds that gave the appearance of something digging them.

The first thought was an animal digging them, but we only had squirrels and various birds who would not perform such a task. I promised myself that henceforth a close watch on this area would be mandated. This was rewarded a few days later when I noted a slightly depressed trail through the earth and what appeared to be paw or claw marks on each side. A day later, from my porch, I spotted a small turtle making its way up the bank leading from the river. When it reached the area of the trails, it stopped and began digging into the dirt forming a small hole. It then backed down into the hole with its head and front paws out over the edge. Then came the surprise of a lifetime. The small female turtle began to lay eggs, nearly a dozen. Upon completion, she crawled out of the nest and covered the eggs with fine dirt. After all was completed, she made her way back into the river, leaving a small mound. This recurred several times over the next two days and the mystery of the mounds was solved.

However, a new puzzle occurred as I noted the egg deposit site was dug up with fragment of egg shells scattered in the debris. I immediately thought, "Some animal has found the nest and eaten the eggs, but there are no other animals around that are able to perform this task. Another mysterious guest is here."

I searched the heavily wooded area hoping to find some sign of the culprit, but to no avail. The diligent search was a failure.

A few more diggings occurred and then none, as all of the nests were destroyed. We were left with an unsolved mystery, until several months later when I returned home from work and Pam greeted me with, "I know what ate our turtle eggs."

With a marked questioning look I replied, "What?"

She walked to the edge of the porch saying, "Come here and I will show you."

I followed her and gazing outside, what to my wandering eyes should appear, but a mother raccoon and three tiny babies following her. We have seen them several times since, but the turtles have never returned to be our strange guests on the bayou.

POEM

Behind our recent assignments
We felt a threat was lurking.
And at our last meeting, it became so real
That it had our heads a 'jerking.
Kim sneaked it in, with all of us surprised,
In a manner none of us innocents ever surmised.

We all sat around as once upon a time,
We all hung loose on a Muscadine vine.
We had given our commencement address
With all the skills that we could possess.

The chatting between ourselves
As we prepared to leave,
Was centered upon a problem
Very difficult to believe.

As I drove home, I thought of the assignment given us by Kim this time.
We had to create a poem and of course the words had to rhyme.
My brain doesn't work that way,
So if I couldn't do it, what would I say?

The drive home became longer
And the difficulty stronger,
As I attempted to put together
My birds of a feather.

After arriving home and informing my wife,
She reminded me that I always excelled in strife.

Why should this task cause such consternation?
When all it took was a bit of information.
However, as the week went by and nothing did appear,
I was afraid of being at class with only my fear.

'Twas the night before writing class
When all through the house,
Not a creature was stirring
As I lay by my spouse.

Millions of thoughts
Kept pouring through my head,
But nothing came out
As though I was dead.

Then suddenly thoughts appeared
That completed my task,
And flooded me with feelings
In which I could bask.

Out of the bed
I jumped with a crash,
And all of the old writing papers
I threw into the trash.

The poem became written with ease and speed,
And the title became obvious indeed.
As I thought of the mouse
When "not a creature was stirring all through the house."

So, thanks to you, Kim
For releasing your whim,
It was quite stimulating
And even a little scintillating.

ACKNOWLEDGEMENTS

I want to send a special thank you to my Life Writing Instructor, Kim Graham, for her excellent teaching and encouragement. Also, thanks go out to all of the members of my writing class who helped by example and encouragement. A special thanks goes to Debbie Breaux and Ana Aucoin for their effort in producing each story. The most special thanks goes out to my daughter, Susan (Cissy) Tabor, without whose help I could never put this all together as a book, and thanks to the support of my daughter Felisa. Finally, my greatest thanks to my wife, Pam, whose constant help was and still is always there.

BIOGRAPHY

Walter H. Daniels, M.D., was born at home in the Cajun village of Gueydan, Louisiana to Homer and Delta Daniels. He graduated from Gueydan High School in 1951 and L.S.U. A&M with a B.S. in 1955. After graduating from LSU Medical School with an M.D. in 1959, he completed training and became board certified as a Family Practitioner. He practiced in Morgan City, Louisiana for fifty-three years.

Dr. Daniels lives along a mossy tree-lined bayou, with his beautiful wife, Pam on Idlewild Plantation in Patterson, Louisiana with their three cats, one sassy dog and possibly more than one ghost.

Made in the USA
San Bernardino, CA
14 January 2017